# Motherhood

*is a contact sport*

*To Erica*

*Yours in motherhood*

*Susan Beirne*

# Other Books from *The Baltimore Sun*:

The Wild Side of Maryland: An Outdoor Guide

The 1996-1997 Maryland Business Almanac

Cal Touches Home

This *Baltimore Sun* book was published by SunSource, the information service of the *Sun*. To order any of the above titles, or for information on research, reprints and information from the paper's archives, please call 410.332.6800.

# Motherhood
## *is a contact sport*

*A collection of the writings of Baltimore Sun columnist*
## Susan Reimer

THE BALTIMORE SUN

Published by
*The Baltimore Sun*
A Times-Mirror Co
501 N. Calvert Street
Baltimore, MD 21278

Layout and design by Jennifer Halbert
Photos of Ms. Reimer by Jim Burger
Chalkboard photo ©1998 PhotoDisc, Inc.
Edited by Ray Frager

Special thanks to the Baltimore Ravens for the football used on the cover. Thanks also to Quill publishing for their permission to reprint excerpts from "A Woman's Life."

ISBN – 0-964-98196-3
Library of Congress Catalog Card Number 98-070956.

Motherhood is a contact sport: a collection of the writings of Baltimore Sun columnist Susan Reimer: a publication of the Baltimore Sun - 1998 - Baltimore, MD: Baltimore Sun Co: 1998

*This collection is dedicated to the memory of my parents, Robert and Jean Reimer.*

*They'd have been so impressed.*

# Contents:

# Introduction

WHEN I WAS in college in the early 1970s, I was a serious, anti-establishment, anti-war type. I sought to get the sports section of the college newspaper for which I worked disbanded as superfluous and irrelevant.

Years later, I would make a name for myself as one of the first women sportswriters in the country.

When I was in college, I believed in serial monogamy. I planned to love a number of really interesting men, one right after the other, so no love relationship I had would grow cold or boring.

Today, I am devoted to my husband, and I have written that unhappy couples should consider staying married for the well-being of their children.

As a college student, I wore no bra, no make-up and my hair tied back in a bandanna. Personal appearance was considered phony window-dressing by us then.

All these years later, I get my hair streaked blond every three months, I broke my tailbone doing aerobics in one of those cute little spandex outfits and I have had a glamour make-over.

When I was in college, I determined that if I ever had children, which I never expected to have, I would continue to work and actively pursue a career. The kids would benefit from having a strong, independent, successful role model of a mother.

But after my second child was born, I returned to work only three days a week and gave up traveling — a decision that pretty much grounded my career as a sportswriter.

When I was a young professional woman, I disdained PTA mothers and homeroom mothers. I could have written the words to the song: "Here's to the girls who play wife.... The ones who follow the rules, and meet themselves at the schools, too busy to know they are fools. Aren't they a gem?" *(From "The Ladies Who Lunch" from "Company," music and lyrics by Stephen Sondheim.)*

Today, I spend so much time in and out of my children's school that some of the kids think I work there.

Eight years ago, I asked *The Sun* to free me to return often to Pittsburgh to help my family care for my dying father. In return, I agreed to work on the sports copy desk, where my help was needed.

I went from crafting my own lovely little sports stories during the day to staying up until 3 a.m. writing headlines on other people's sports stories.

I did not sleep during those years on the copy desk. I was the perfect housewife during the day and the dutiful, though very tired, copy editor at night.

But I missed writing, and so I wrote "Members of the Wedding" for *Sun Magazine* and a couple of essays for the Perspective section of the Sunday paper. They were all about my family life, and my editor and friend, Marty Kaiser, asked if I thought I could write a column about just such things.

It was July 1993. I took a deep breath and said, "Yes."

Now, I am working during the day again, but the column is consuming, so I am no longer a very good housewife. I have a cleaning lady and my sitter handles most of the wash. My kids must occasionally feed themselves or go hungry. And my husband makes the beds and cleans up the breakfast dishes without my even asking.

The point of all of this, if it has a point, is that I am not who I thought I would be. Not who I planned to be. Not who I wanted to be.

Instead, I am the woman I once ridiculed. The car-pooling mom, driving Little Leaguers around in a station wagon, fixing treats for school parties and endlessly debating school issues with other mothers.

And, for heaven's sake, writing about it all.

Men, I think, plan their lives degree by degree and job by job, as if they are marching toward some known point in the future. Men seem to lead one life, in a straight line.

Women lead many lives, and the course they follow keeps getting bumped in another direction, usually by family concerns.

I'd like to share a passage from Susan Cheever's nonfiction account of the life of one of my contemporaries. The book is called: "A Woman's Life: The Story of an Ordinary American and Her Extraordinary Generation."

Susan Cheever is writing about herself here, but she might be writing about me.

> "Although more than 80 percent of women with school-age children work, they earn less than 70 percent for each dollar earned by their male co-workers. There is clear unfairness here, but the real unfairness is built deep into our social system and is less visibly offensive. Often, very often, women have to choose

between careers and family in a way that most men don't. A woman's career, once she has a husband and children, has a kind of conditional mood to it because there is no doubt which is more important in the crunch — a job or a child.

"As almost every day requires a choice between kids and work — with illnesses requiring trips to the pediatrician, school conferences and performances, social crises and run-of-the-mill clinginess — the purity of a woman's commitment to work is eroded beyond repair. Women have had to find another foundation for work in our generation and that foundation is usually our children's financial needs.

"Even writing makes this requirement. I'm writing with a fraction of my mind on each of my two children and I'm writing in time literally snatched from their needs. My work competes every moment with the sweet, scary, sacred obligations to my children.

"Does this competition make it better? Am I a better mother because I have another source for my identity and my sense of self than my children? I would say, yes. My children would say, no."

But this is OK with me. I like my life, crazy as it is. It is the product of all the things that have happened to me. It is a distillation of all the choices I have made and all that choices that have been forced on me. But it is not at all what I wanted for myself, what I would have predicted for myself.

If someone had told me when I was that college firebrand that I would one day car-pool baseball players and murmur silent prayers outside a ballet audition — and that I would make my living writing about that stuff — I would have laughed out loud.

If someone had told me when my son was born that it would be 10 years until I had a job in which I could again feel such pride, I would have wept.

The world of sports was my world for 14 years and it has a platitude for every occasion, including this one: Life never follows your game plan, no matter how carefully you prepare it. So live on the balls of your feet and be ready to move, because when the whistle blows, the next play may be coming your way.

# Chapter 1

# Hello,
*it's me*

# A brand new ballgame

"DAD? I'M IN the press box at Yankee Stadium."

I cupped my hand over the phone, barely able to contain the excitement I knew it would be unprofessional to reveal. Bob Reimer's oldest daughter was covering an Orioles-Yankees series from that storied place.

"Will they show you on TV?" he asked, and I could hear him smiling.

"Oh, Dad," I said, exasperated.

*The Sun* had hired me as a sportswriter just months before, and sent me to an important — and emotional — baseball series that weekend in New York. It was August 1979, Yankees catcher Thurman Munson had just died in an airplane crash, and it was my job to capture the grief of his teammates.

I could not wait to tell my father. The first of four daughters, each of whom had shown less inclination toward athletics than the one before, was writing about sports. He could not have been more thrilled if the doctor had said, "Mr. Reimer, it's a boy."

Growing up poor on a farm in New Kensington, Pa., my father escaped into sports from the burden of supporting a widowed mother. He once played golfing legend Arnold Palmer in an amateur tournament near his home — and family legend has it that my father beat him.

He was an excellent tennis player, too. And charming enough to talk his way into the elite country clubs of Western Pennsylvania, even if he didn't have the change in his pocket to tip the locker room attendant.

When I chose a career in journalism, he was circumspect. Teaching or nursing made more sense for a woman, the better to fit wage-earning around a family. The notion of a career didn't seem very practical to the father of girls.

Nor did he understand the nature of the business. When I passed some of my news stories from the student newspaper at Ohio University to my father to hand off to a friend who might be able to help me get a job, he handed them back.

"This stuff doesn't sound like you," he said. "I don't see any of you in this."

I was furious. I wasn't trying to be Emily Dickinson. I was trying to be Bob Woodward. And, sometimes, I was trying to be Red Smith.

Working in Pittsburgh, I had just a taste of sportswriting, doing feature stories on the championship teams of the 1970s — the Pirates, the Super Bowl Steelers, Pitt with Tony Dorsett and Dan Marino. For *The Sun*, I would try it full time.

My decision to write sports at once delighted and baffled my father. What did I know about sports?

Over the years, I mailed my father the evidence. Envelopes arrived in Pittsburgh from World Series cities, Super Bowls, Sugar Bowls, Triple Crown races, and from Newport, R.I., and the America's Cup.

I was in love when the Orioles lost to Pittsburgh in the 1979 World Series — Mr. Right was covering the Pirates — and I was the only pregnant reporter in the press box when they beat the Philadelphia Phillies in 1983.

When my son, Joseph, was born, NFL Commissioner Pete Rozelle sent flowers, and Baltimore Colts coach Frank Kush sent a $1 million player contract dated 2006. A million dollars wouldn't buy a backup lineman at today's free-agent prices.

Joe was a month old in March 1984 when the Colts left town. If I didn't know it when Joe was born, I knew then that my life had changed for good and always.

Two years later, Jessica arrived and I stopped jumping onto airplanes. There were no more glamorous datelines in the clippings sent home to Pittsburgh. I think that disappointed my father, although he never spoke of it to me. When he died, I wrote the eulogy for his funeral — the toughest assignment I would ever draw.

Now the sports that fill my days are 8-and-under swimming races, soccer and Little League baseball. The only traveling I do is to the fields, gyms and pools around Anne Arundel County. My years covering sports have made me the scorekeeper at my children's games. The best reporting I do is to their grandparents.

I am a car-pooling mother of two, I tell people, and I work for a newspaper in my spare time. Like the athletes I have written about, I have had to make a life after the games are over. This is my life now, and writing about it is the easiest writing I have ever done. The most fun, too. I think my father would say, after all these years, that this stuff finally sounds like me.

# Life in Mars

I HAVE BEEN to Mars and back, and I can say for certain that there is life there.

It is not the single-cell, microbiotic life scientists think existed 3.6 billion years ago on the hot rock that is our next-door neighbor in the solar system. It is the kind of life you find in a small town.

Mars, Pa., is 18 miles from Pittsburgh, and my sister discovered life there 20 years ago. She and her young husband stumbled on an affordable house in Mars, beyond the suburban sprawl that continues to grow out from the city.

The children born to her there are in full adolescent flower now, and she says she would fear their growing up anywhere but in the atmosphere of Mars. "I know they are missing out on some things here," Ellen says. "But I wouldn't raise kids anywhere else."

They are missing out on Playstation, my son declared, as we settled in for a week with Aunt Ellen. The next generation in video game technology had not made it to Mars, he said, confounded.

"They don't know about lettuce spinners, either," I said to him in a stage whisper. I discovered that when I sought a small hostess gift for my sister's kitchen.

But Mars has a flying saucer in its tiny town square, spray-painted silver and looking like something out of a bad 1950s movie.

"Mars likes to laugh at itself, doesn't it, Mom?" said Joe as we walked each morning to the grocery store to buy the fixings for that night's dinner. (No check-cashing card required. The women at the checkout know everyone who lives in Mars.)

Joe was right. Mars does have a sense of humor about itself. The midget football teams are named the Martians, the Astros and the Rockets. The high school team is called the Planets. The motto of the Mars Bank is "Our service is out of this world," and it is stamped on each check near a logo of a planet ringed with swirling gases.

"When I worked in Pittsburgh in the 1970s, I couldn't cash a check," my sister remembers. "They'd take one look and think it was a gag."

There is only one Mars, though the atlas lists a couple of Venuses and a few Jupiters. Some say that it was named by the wife of the town's

4

first resident, Samuel Parks, in 1873. She was a student of astronomy. Others say it is named for Samuel Marshall, a judge who established the community's first post office.

Mars — the small town — is discovered again every time the red planet makes the news. When the Viking satellite landed on the planet in 1976, the town sold thousands of red soil samples for $1 each, dug from the brick yard near town. Tens of thousands of letters were mailed to Mars that year, requesting a postmark. T-shirts, bumper stickers, caps and postcards sold wildly.

When this latest news was announced — that primitive, microscopic life may have been found on a meteorite that came from Mars and landed in Antarctica 13,000 years ago — *People* magazine and the BBC discovered Mars again.

But you have to stay in Mars longer than it takes to get a sound bite or a gimmicky picture to enjoy the "Andy of Mayberry" quality of it, to feel your pulse slow to the pace of life there.

When Interstate 79 made its way north, it had a Mars exit for a time and the residents of Mars, shrunk now to 1,700, thought for sure they would be overrun by colonizing city dwellers. But the name of the exit was changed and Mars drifted back into its anonymous quietude.

In Mars, residents still pick up their mail at Judge Marshall's post office in what serves as downtown. City fathers won't allow home delivery, fearing the heart of town will stop beating if people do not have to visit it.

That is hard for anyone who has eaten at Howard's cafe to imagine. Howard likes to cook, and so he is at his grill every morning at 4, putting together his $1.99 breakfast special. And nothing tastes as good for lunch as Howard's hot roast beef sandwich with french fries and gravy. $2.25.

Mars is not big enough for a stoplight, though it has a blinking red one. You can hear the whistle of the CSX train at 5 a.m. and again at 5 p.m. A rabbit takes the same path through the neighbor's yard and into my sister's garden every evening at dusk. My sister knows that because, in Mars, you spend the evening on your front porch sipping coffee while the kids race around on their bikes or draw on the street with chalk.

People leave their car keys in the ignition overnight and their front doors open for a midnight breeze in Mars. No one distrusts his neighbor. I have a sister who locks her doors when she takes a shower. Ellen only locks her doors when she leaves on vacation.

On her 40th birthday, Ellen's husband painted a huge sign for her and stuck it right in the middle of downtown Mars. "Happy Birthday, Ellen" was all it said. But throughout the day, the people of Mars wished my sister a happy birthday. They knew who "Ellen" was.

"Rudi just laughs at John," Ellen says, speaking of the differences between our street-smart, city-boy nephew and her son. "Rudi wouldn't trust a stranger with his real name. John would trust a stranger with his wallet."

Joe, too, is city-wise. On one of our evening walks, he saw a little boy playing with a puppy while a little girl rode a swing nearby. "Oh, Mom. This is too much," he said. "I don't believe what I am seeing. In our neighborhood, it would be some guy walking a pit bull with a spiked collar."

"Joe," I said, laughing. "You exaggerate."

"OK. Maybe not that bad. But I feel like Aunt Ellen lives back in time."

No, Joe, I think. It is like she lives on another planet.

# Welfare at ground level

IN HIS STATE of the Union speech last week, President Clinton repeated his promise to end welfare as we know it. I hope he is successful, because welfare as I know it is a dreadful life for any family.

I don't know welfare firsthand. I don't even know it secondhand. My friends and family have managed to keep their heads above water in this shrinking economy, though we all know that we are one corporate downsizing away from disaster.

But I live in a city, and my children go to school with children whose families are on welfare or who live in subsidized housing. Most of what I know about such poverty I have learned as only a spectator, but what I see is depressing beyond words.

I listen to politicians, and even some of my well-meaning friends, talk about these families as if they were comfortable and content at the expense of the rest of us, as if someone would connive and maneuver to live the kind of life welfare families live.

And I have often thought about these politicians and my well-meaning friends and how long they would last on welfare, in poverty. How long they would continue to be hopeful and optimistic. How long it would be before their spirits were crushed. I know I would not last 10 minutes.

Just the logistics of poverty would defeat me, and, quite frankly, it would defeat most of the men and women I know.

Imagine if you did not have a checking account because you could not afford all the banking fees, and so every time you cashed a check, someone took a piece of it for their trouble. That would also mean that you had to pay all of your bills in cash, and that would mean, of course, that you had to travel to the store or utility to do so.

Then imagine that you did not have a car. Not just for a day while it is being tuned, but forever.

No car means grocery shopping is even more of a hassle. No car means sick children in the middle of a school day or trips to the emergency room are even more frightening. No car means after-school activities for your kids or volunteering in the classroom or night meetings or band concerts at school are beyond even an honest effort.

7

Now put no car together with no washer or dryer and see what kind of mood you are in.

How about unresponsive landlords? Or suspicious social workers? Or slow-moving bureaucrats? What if these are the people with whom you must negotiate daily?

What if they would not deliver pizza to your neighborhood? What if you had no phone to call them in any case because you did not have the cash for the large security deposit the phone company requires?

This is just the minor stuff, the annoying logistics of poverty. There are other things about welfare that I hope never to know.

My husband works so late so often that I have said to him that when he is not part of the solution, he is part of the problem. What if he never came home at all?

No paycheck. No dad to coach my daughter or to teach my son to draw and paint. No one to take over the role of taskmaster when I am weary. No shoulder on which to spill my tears.

How would I feel if the same people who praise a middle-class woman for staying home to raise her children considered me lazy and irresponsible when I did?

For welfare families, there is often no money for such basics as food or medical attention. What if there was no money for the extras that families such as mine take for granted? For dance lessons, soccer camps or Christmas?

What if my children chose to go hungry at school rather than accept the free lunch that would identify them to all their friends as poor?

Worse by far: What if the world had already given up on my children? Doomed my son to drugs and crime, my daughter to early pregnancy and single-motherhood. What if people crossed the street when they saw my son coming instead of stopping me to tell me what a beautiful child he is?

And what if the Republican Congress had its way and ordered me to work but did not provide me with medical insurance? How would I pay for my son's asthma medicine without the coverage I had when I was jobless and on welfare?

What if the Republican Congress had its way and ordered me to work but did not provide any money for decent child care so that I spent my 3-to-11 p.m. shift worrying about my kids, home alone or with someone I could not trust?

What if I could not convince my children that four years of college and thousands of dollars in student loans was the right path, and the easy, dangerous money of the streets was not?

And what if I had no hope to make all my children's dreams come true, from video games and American Girl dolls to art school or graduate school?

What if teachers or shopkeepers or neighbors or social workers or the politicians in Washington looked at my children and simply assumed that I did not love them the way they love their children? That I was an inattentive or undisciplined parent, that I had no values to teach them, no control over their behavior, no care for their future.

I hope President Clinton and the Republican Congress can find some way to end welfare as I know it. I know little enough. I am sure the women who live this life could paint a more detailed and unpleasant picture.

How can the politicians and my well-meaning friends believe that any woman would choose this life for her children? How can they judge and argue and stubbornly refuse to help her?

# A pretend Christmas

IT WASN'T THE Christmas decorations that surprised me when I walked into a mall in the days just after Halloween. It was how I felt when I saw them. Not sad. Sick.

Not sickened, as in annoyed or disgusted. Sick. My head felt light and my legs unsteady. There was a wave of nausea, followed by a rush of adrenaline as I tried not to pass out.

In that way we have of inspecting our lives as we live them, I watched myself from outside myself as I fought off what felt like flu symptoms.

"Odd," I thought, detached, observing. "Grief manifesting itself as morning sickness. I don't remember reading that in any of the pamphlets at the funeral home."

There will be so many people missing from Christmas this year that it is hard to keep track of the different kinds of sadness I will feel. My mother. My husband's father. My husband's good friend, Mike. All died within 12 remarkable days in August.

"I don't know why we are even having Christmas," said my daughter, Jessie, who is 10. "Everybody is dead."

After completing most of her Christmas shopping, she announced: "If I die, just remember that I love everyone and the presents are in my bedroom closet."

She is just one of those around me who will need customized comforting this Christmas.

It is hard to know where to begin, what to say to whom, how I feel myself.

The grieving books say that the holidays are painful not only for the absence of those we love, but also because there is such a contrast between what we are supposed to feel and what we really feel, between the holiday bustle around us and our own feelings of tremendous fatigue. Grief is exhausting. I don't seem to have the energy for the rituals that my children are used to, the ones that will signal to them that their mother is OK.

What we don't have at the holidays is what we need most. Silence, solitude, a time to reflect, remember, recover and plan some kind of future without the ones we love.

Our sadness is accompanied by anxiety and confusion about how we are supposed to celebrate without appearing happy. Someone told me that you never send Christmas cards in the year of a death and that you decorate only modestly. I had never heard that, and my first thought was to ask the one person who would know. My mother.

All around my family are people who are unsure how to approach us, what to say or what to do. And I find myself wondering how to reassure them, how to let them know that we are basically OK and we will not shatter if they ask about our sadness and we will understand if they cannot bring themselves to ask.

The literature on grief is full of advice about the holidays, but grief knows no calendar and we are ambushed by pain every day, not just on the days when the banks and stores are closed. I am just as likely to be stabbed by a memory while pulling on my socks as I am sitting in church on Christmas Eve.

We can console ourselves with new traditions, we are told, that commemorate the missing loved one. Light a tribute candle, plan a group visit to the gravesite, leave a single flower at their place at the holiday dinner table, offer a toast.

That may work for some, but I cannot do such tender things because I know a wave of emotion would sweep me away. My children, for whom I must model grief and composure in the most searing balancing act of my parenthood, would be terrified by the tears that would follow such tributes.

Even so, we are advised to have a plan, any plan, for the holiday season, so we will not be startled into fresh grief by something unexpected.

This is my plan: I will pretend.

My husband's father, my children's gentle grandpa, would always leave in the middle of the Christmas morning chaos to usher at church. He would search through the piles of presents and wrapping paper for his new Christmas socks and his new Christmas suspenders and then he would exit for Mass just as his grandchildren's excitement reached an uncomfortable decibel level.

I will pretend that Grandpa isn't back from church yet.

Mike and my husband were runnin' buddies in the days when they were regularly unsuccessful with women, and it has always been the joke that Libby and I rescued them from a life of idiosyncratic bachelorhood.

There is a picture in our photo album of these two men standing proudly behind their pregnant wives, and Mike and Gary settled into exemplary fatherhood. Mike's only carry-over indulgence was his love of ice cream. He could eat more of it faster than anyone you ever met. When we would visit Mike and Libby and their four boys, Mike would go out for buckets of ice cream and return to sit down among us with a mixing bowl full of the stuff.

I will pretend that Mike is out buying ice cream.

Christmas Eve has always been spent with my family, and my parents never seemed happier than when their four daughters, their four sons-in-law and their 11 grandchildren finally left.

They had a diminishing capacity for the noise of so many yapping daughters and squealing kids, and they often seemed overwhelmed by the confusion as my sisters and I scurried about, barking at children, serving food and teasing each other acidly. We would hardly notice our quiet parents until it was time to leave, and then there would be kisses and hugs all around.

This Christmas I will pretend that my mom and my dad are there with us as always. Waiting patiently, lovingly, for us to say goodbye.

# A level playing field

IN 1979, BASEBALL held a very different kind of Opening Day. Under threat of court action, Major League Baseball opened its clubhouses to women sportswriters, thanks to Melissa Ludtke of *Sports Illustrated*, who had run point for a very small group of women in a suit against the New York Yankees.

That summer was my first as a sportswriter for *The Sun*. At the time, I was covering just about everything except baseball, but my editor sent me to the Orioles the next day anyway. In essence, my assignment was to create an incident and then write about it.

When I and two other women arrived at the Orioles clubhouse, that sacred place where players change and eat and play cards and talk among themselves — and with male sportswriters — Earl Weaver, then the manager of the Orioles, met us at the door.

We would not be allowed in unless we had notes from our fathers, he said.

That was 15 years ago. And so I could not help but smile when the Orioles asked this off-season if I would appear in an instructional video on media relations — a cameo appearance to explain to the players the role of women sportswriters.

In my videotaped segment, I explained that women become sportswriters for pretty much the same reason men do. They like sports, and they like to write. Women sportswriters think there are really good stories out there in the world of sports, and they want a chance to write them.

I explained that women sportswriters want to be in the locker rooms and clubhouses because that's where the athletes are. And, more important, perhaps, that is where the male sportswriters are. And if the men sportswriters can talk to the athletes there, the women can, too. Women are asking for a level playing field, for the same rules to apply to both teams. That is something the athletes should find easy to understand, I said.

Do women like it in the locker rooms? No. They are as uncomfortable in there as athletes are to have them there, maybe more. They want to get their quotes and get out.

How do women want athletes to treat them? Like an athlete would want somebody to treat his sister or his wife or his girlfriend. With dignity and respect. No balls of tape thrown at the back of the head. No naked moon shots or foul language sent in their direction.

During 14 years as a sportswriter, I had experiences that made me cry, made me sick and made me stay in bed with the covers over my head. Funny thing. Few of them happened inside a locker room or a clubhouse.

Weaver, the Orioles manager who wanted a note from my father, certainly never would have said the things he once said to me if my father were listening. One afternoon — outside, near the Orioles dugout — he turned to me and demanded to know my sexual orientation, or whether I had any sexual appetite at all. He did it in front my colleagues and in language that would have made, well, made a ballplayer blush.

When I was obviously pregnant with my first child and covering the then-Baltimore Colts, running back Curtis Dickey interrupted my interview with another player — taking place in a hallway — to say, "You been getting some, huh, girl."

Those incidents told me that the treatment of women sportswriters by athletes and managers had very little to do with where they were standing or which one was changing clothes.

To their credit, the Orioles have addressed the strain that exists for women in their clubhouse. But there is irony in my appearance in their video because I was one of the women they had tried to keep out all those years ago. Here we are, all these years later, and women are still explaining why they want to be sportswriters.

We are explaining it to a new generation of athletes, to be sure. Guys who were in grade school when we were starting in this business. But it struck me that we are still explaining it. And that we will probably still be explaining our presence in any nontraditional field 10 years hence. That maybe we will forever be explaining what we are doing, not just in the locker room, but in the work force.

There will be several women sportswriters in the press box when the Orioles open their season today. The good news is, none will be required to present a note from her father. The bad news is, these women, and many more of us, will be required to explain again and again why it is we work.

# Parentness is close to Godliness

SUNDAY SCHOOL HAS started, and so has the whining.

My son, who has never cared what time it was before, now wears a watch on Sundays so he knows when Sunday school is almost over. My daughter goes along peacefully only because they sell doughnuts before classes begin.

It's boring. Why do you make us go? they demand.

The argument I had always heard — considering all that God has done for you, particularly in the area of worldly possessions, an hour of your time isn't much to ask in return — has left no impression. So I tried a new approach. "Why do you think I go?" I asked them. "Nobody is making me go."

They were struck dumb. For once, no smart-mouthed answers.

No easy answers, either. But it is certainly true that something about children brings us face to face with God.

Maybe it is the miracle of their safe arrival. Maybe it is because when we feel that uncontainable, unconditional love for them, it becomes easier to comprehend that there might indeed be a Heavenly Father who feels that way about us.

Maybe it is all the Faustian deals we make over our children. Keep them safe, God. Let me live until they are raised, God, and you can have anything you want in return.

Ask your friends why they take their children to church or temple. For some, there was never a question but that they would pass their faith on to their children. For others, the arrival of children has meant wakeful nights wrestling with the confused and possibly unhappy religious messages they carried forward from their own youth. And it starts right away: Will there be a baptism? In which church?

Notice, too, that it is probably the women whom you are asking. Mothers tend to be the prime movers in the spiritual and emotional lives of their children.

"Having grown up with it, it seemed natural that it would be the thing for my kids, too," a friend says to me.

"Most traditional religions provide an external authority for all the things you tell your kids anyway — it is not just your mother saying so, but thousands of years and some pretty holy books say so, too.

"And it is another community of support, both on a practical and spiritual level, for your children."

She had a much longer term and more positive experience with organized religion than her husband had. But she knew that if she was going to get him inside a holy building, it had to be his holy building. And so she converted.

(My Catholic husband was only half-kidding when he said: "If we are going to take them to church, it had better be the one, true church.")

"He would have been more than reluctant," she says. "It didn't feel like such a big deal to me. I was just changing how I was expressing myself."

And so it has been she who has guided the children through their religious education, reminded them of the holy days and packed them all off to services.

But beside her is a husband who put aside any unhappy baggage from his own religious training on the unspoken agreement that both mother and father need to be models of faith for their children. It doesn't count if you send the kids with Mom, or just drop them off at Sunday school while you go to brunch. The kids will call you on that hypocrisy.

"And it gives them a sense of history, too," she says. "A sense that they are part of something that began thousands of years ago and will continue into the future."

She knows she might simply be giving her children something to reject during an inevitable period of adolescent rebellion. That they might walk away from the religious traditions she lovingly keeps.

"I don't visualize a flat-out rejection," she says. "The pressure has never been that great to go. I have never made it an issue of force.

"And if they choose another faith, I can even handle that," she says. "So long as it is something tolerant and inclusive."

She hopes they will look back on their childhood as a period punctuated by religious observances that were special, happy, family times. That if they choose not to be part of a religious community, they will at least be able to look back and find some value — and some values — from their religious education.

"And if they drift away from it?" she says, repeating the question. "I'll bide my time and see what happens."

Just wait, I say. Wait until they have children.

# Three seats, two kids, a vehicle of summer memories

"TWELVE LUNCHES TO pack, 10 lunches to pack, eight lunches to pack. . . ." That is how I counted down the last days of the school year in June, days that felt like they, too, were jammed into a brown paper sack.

The calendar was cluttered with year-end assemblies, meetings and recitals. The kids had lost their self-control as the hours of their confinement dwindled.

And my throat was a little tighter every morning as I anticipated a summer of two-on-one. Them against me.

If hell truly is a punishment of our own making, then I know what eternal damnation will be for me. Two kids in a car and a list of errands. That's how I spent my summer vacation.

My children are at that awkward age — too old to be helplessly buckled down in car seats, too young to be left at home alone. And so we took out the frustrations of a long, hot summer on each other in the air-conditioned comfort of a station wagon.

Your children's shortcomings are much more evident — especially to each other — in the confines of an automobile. The picking and the bickering. ("He touched me." "She looked at me.") My station wagon has a third seat, and now I know why. The seat behind the driver had to function as a kind of DMZ, made necessary when one whipped a seat belt — buckle first — at the other.

The car became a rolling landfill, too, littered with the refuse of a hundred good-behavior bribes, the waste of endless begging in public places, the leftovers of a hundred drive-through lunches.

The bickering ceased only long enough for a little four-wheel-drive "Jeopardy." "Can infinity ants lift an elephant?" "Is the sun shining out in space?" Buzzz. Jessie, for $200, reproductive biology. . . . "How do you get twins?"

"Mommy can't talk while she drives," I said. "Are we there yet?" was starting to sound good.

17

But that car carried my children and me through a summer of transitions, too. And when I pull out the mental snapshots from this summer, my throat tightens again. But this time, not with tension.

That car carried Joe, 9 years old and with a new buzz cut that took away his baby-fine blond locks, to wrestling camp at the Naval Academy. When I watched him walk off the mat, face streaked with dirty sweat, T-shirt sleeves rolled up to show off miniature biceps, I blinked hard in disbelief. As he came toward me, hips rolling with the bow-legged swagger of an athlete, he looked 14.

The car took Jessie to swim team every morning. She started with a doggie paddle, but by summer's end, she could complete an individual medley — four different strokes strung brutally together. She raced with some steel in her I didn't know she had. She was no baby anymore.

The kids fell asleep more than once in that car, and they did not wake as they were carried up to bed. They slept the thick, heavy sleep of summer, exhausted by play. Not the fitful, anxious sleep of the school year, when dreams of playground bullies and spelling tests left them tangled in their covers.

Cradled up the steps, they smelled vaguely of chlorine, sweetly of sweat. The bottoms of their dangling feet were as brown as their tanned shoulders from a night of catching fireflies barefoot.

If you are patient on those sticky summer nights, you can watch your children grow while they sleep. And so that box of school clothes packed away in June might just as well stay there. Blue jeans are inches too short. And it would not be the first day of school without a brand new pair of tennis shoes.

My husband says that if kids are excited by the purchase of school supplies, you are winning the education battle. That may be wishful thinking, but there were few fights in the car when back-to-school stuff was on our list of errands.

There is something about a new tablet, a pristine school box, bright pink erasers and the smell of freshly sharpened pencils that seems so full of possibilities.

And so I gave them a lift to the first day of school in the station wagon. Joe started fourth grade, and I think the gloves come off this year. Teachers don't pull you onto their laps when you are having a bad day in the fourth grade. They will expect him to be organized and to work independently, God help him.

Jessie is in second grade, and the shy uncertainty of a first-grader in a new school is gone. She wants to walk home with her cat pack of girlfriends this year, and I am not allowed to kiss her goodbye on school property.

Where was I on that first day of school? At the grocery store, alone.

# Who do you think you are?

A FRIEND WHO is also a doctor says she worries sometimes that administrators at the medical school from which she graduated will find the rest of her application behind a file cabinet, see what a mediocre student she is certain that she was and revoke her degree.

A friend who works for the Environmental Protection Agency and who has a wall covered with awards and a pocketful of bonus checks for exemplary work is convinced her bosses will ask for it all back. She can't be that good, she thinks, because she works part time.

A friend who has been elevated to a pedestal by all the mothers who envy her good sense and her calm in a storm is just waiting for all these admirers to show up at 5:30 on just about any weeknight and watch her lose it with one of her children.

A friend who is an artist is sure one of her old professors will walk through the door at one of her showings and say loudly enough for every guest to hear: "Art? What makes you think this is art? Didn't you learn anything?"

These women and many more of us are suffering from the Impostor Syndrome, a neurosis first labeled by Dr. Pauline Rose Clance in 1978. She found a pattern of fear among people who secretly believe they have been overestimated and will, at any moment, be found out.

I thought it was just me.

"It runs deeper than not being able to accept a compliment," said the idealized mother. "Why do we insist on focusing on those moments when we are not living out other people's perceptions of us?"

Dr. Clance found this Impostor Syndrome in perfectionists who could never meet their own standards. And she found that this attitude existed among men, too. But why does it remind me of every woman I know?

Women who don't believe their own reviews. Women who don't believe they deserve their success — who are certain they will be unmasked at any moment. Women who don't feel good after meeting a challenge, who feel as if they simply have fooled everybody one more time.

It is not that they fear success — in the sense that the college women Matina Horner studied were found to fear that success would make them unattractive to men. These are successful women who can't enjoy that success. These are not shy women. These are achieving, often driven women who don't believe they deserve the fruits of their success.

A man I know who has earned nothing but praise and raises for the work he does and for the attitude he brings to the office keeps nothing personal at his desk. No coffee mug, no family pictures. He says he doesn't want to have to pack up after they fire him. Men can feel like impostors, too. But there is something in the way women are raised that makes them particularly vulnerable to this feeling.

All these years after Simone de Beauvoir wrote that women do everything they can to avoid the strain of an authentic existence, success still frightens us. It opens up all sorts of scary possibilities: responsibilities, power, money. If you already feel you do not deserve the money you make, that you cannot do well the job you have, more money and a promotion only make you feel that much more certain that your house of cards will fall in at the slightest breath.

Any success is risky. And risk is so scary for women that some will do anything to avoid it. Including retreating into their homes.

We are all tired and resentful after a day at the office and a night in the laundry room. Do you ever wonder why we cling to these domestic tasks whether or not we have cooperative husbands and helpful children?

Could it be that this fog of exhaustion is a smoke screen for our conflict? When we are finally unmasked for the frauds that we are in the workplace, at least there will be a job waiting for us at home.

Unless, of course, you are already there.

"I feel like I am acting the part of a mother," said a friend. "Like I am going through the motions of what a good mother is supposed to be. I feel like I am watching myself do it, and my mother or my pediatrician is going to call me on it."

I thought it was only me.

I thought I was the only one who waited in dread for the day when guys in ties come to me and say, "We're sorry, but there has been a mistake. We didn't want you to be a newspaper columnist.

"We wanted you to be a newspaper carrier."

# Healthy choice

RECENTLY, SOME PEOPLE who are not my girlfriends gathered to say nice things about my work, and I insisted that my children dress up in clothes they do not find comfortable and come along to witness it.

I wanted them to have a vision of my career that was not "leaving all day only to come home in a bad mood and make a sorry dinner," which is how my son describes my work life.

It was a lovely ceremony, and I was delighted with my children's good behavior, because you never know how these things are going to go.

On the way home, I thanked my children for being there for me and asked them for their thoughts. They were underwhelmed.

Jessie was baffled by much of the ceremony. Joseph's commentary amounted to: "Yeah, well. Whatever."

I decided that I was a long way from leaving footsteps in which my children would follow.

Jessie has declared that she wants to be a kindergarten teacher. Joe has made no career plans, and I fear he will be living at home and playing computer games until he inherits the house we live in.

But they have seen the underbelly of working motherhood, and I think they have taken in all its lessons. Joe may insist that the mother of his children stay home and raise them, and Jessie may choose that path for herself.

This is one of the side effects of feminism and of women entering the work force: Our children are watching, and they don't like what they see — the fatigue, the frustration, the guilt and sometimes the divorce.

I am more likely to be a role model for some female high school newspaper editor I have never met than for my own kids.

Our own children have not seen much evidence that women can easily fit a career around a marriage and motherhood. The strain in our voices as we urge them to hurry is their first clue. We are doing two things and feeling that we do neither one of them well, and our children can read that in our faces. To my children, I am not a heroine of social change; I am half nuts.

We had better be prepared for the day when they repudiate our choices by making different ones.

Every little girl wants to be a teacher. I wanted to be a teacher. My mother told me to be a teacher because it was something that would fit well around children. Jessie might be just another little girl who wants to be a teacher, or she might have made a decision she cannot yet articulate: It is a job that fits well around children.

It will hurt me if her career or her decisions about family and children are made in reaction against what I have done. But do I want her to think that I have raised the bar and anything less from her will disappoint me? No. Would I want her to fight the battles of a woman in a nontraditional career that I fought for many years as a sportswriter? No.

What I do want for both of my children is the baseline early feminists wanted for women: financial independence and equal opportunity to achieve it. Whether it occurs in a kindergarten classroom, a football press box or in the home office next to the baby's room cannot matter to me.

Those of us who made choices different from our mothers have been searching all our working lives for a validation of that choice, for evidence that we did the right thing, a good thing.

But our daughters and our sons may not see the fight we fought as the good fight. We should start now to find some comfort inside ourselves, because we may not see it reflected in the choices our children make.

# Members of the wedding

"WHERE IS THE long thing that comes off the back?" my 6-year-old daughter, Jessie, asked as she looked at the pictures of a simple civil wedding.

"Where are the girls that are all dressed alike?"

It was not that kind of wedding, I tried to explain.

But she was unconvinced. Nope. That's not what weddings look like. She could not have formed the question, but her confusion was clear: Are you sure you are married?

Ten years is worth celebrating. It's not 25 and it's not 50. But when you have to arrange your children's play dates around the visitation schedules of their friends' fathers, you start to think you ought to celebrate while there is still cause.

"How would you feel about renewing our vows in church?" I said to the man to whom I've been married for 10 years.

"Can I get back to you on that?" Gary said. "Or better yet, I'll have my lawyer call your lawyer."

"You know," I said evenly, firmly, "this is an emotional kind of thing. If I start down this road and you are not right there with me, I could feel real foolish."

"I know," he said, and his voice was kind. But he would not acknowledge the emotional blackmail in what I had said. "Just tell me what time."

And so I began planning the Wedding of the Decade. Our decade, anyway. The bride would wear white. Very Hillary, actually. A double-breasted suit-dress with kick pleats at the knee.

"Where is the long thing that comes off the back?" Jessie asked again. Again, I tried to explain that it was not that kind of wedding. "Oh," she said, suddenly serious. "Can't you 'ford it?"

A sobering question, indeed. But I brightened when she asked me. Here, then, was my wedding partner. If the man of my dreams could not muster any enthusiasm for this kind of planning, the girl of my dreams clearly could.

"Should we have a wedding cake?" I asked. "How about flowers?..." And so we were off.

"I'd like the nosegays to be made of silk flowers," I told the lady in

23

the flower shop. "My daughter is a Barbie kind of girl. She's into costuming, and this will be the ultimate accessory. Her heart would be broken if the flowers died the next day."

The lady in the flower shop had a British accent, a very refined manner and a diploma on the wall written in Japanese. She asked to see the dresses to know the style and color. She asked to see my daughter, to see just how strawberry-blond her hair was.

The flower designs she chose were very sophisticated, very European. And very expensive.

But then she said, "It is quite wonderful working with women renewing their vows. I do a lot of those kinds of weddings, actually, and women like you always know exactly what you want," and I handed her my credit card.

She is perhaps the best caterer in Annapolis, and chocolate cakes are her specialty. So rich they can make your teeth hurt.

"I'm sorry," I said politely. "It will have to be vanilla. I know, that sounds so common. But there is someone in the wedding party who can't eat chocolate."

Won't eat chocolate. My 9-year-old son, Joe. Only kid in America who hates chocolate. It was Jessie who reminded me.

"What about Joe, Mom?" she asked.

"But it can still have people on top," Jessie said.

We did it right the first time, I'd always thought, just barely beating Baltimore's last "Blizzard of the Century" in February 1983. Minutes after our plane took off, they closed the airport.

We were married by a Denver judge in the law offices of a friend. And then we skied a week in Aspen and a week in Vail. We rose at 7 a.m. every day to ski the bumps and the fresh powder and then retired to outdoor hot tubs, sipping wine while the evening's snowfall dusted our hair.

This time, it would be much more tame. A weekend at a bed-and-breakfast in Harpers Ferry, W.Va. The Civil War for him, antiques for her.

There would be no music, seeing as there was no organ or piano in the Priests' Chapel above the sanctuary at St. Mary's Church in Annapolis. "That's OK. It's not that kind of wedding," I said.

But my dearest friend called to offer the services of her children. Amanda, the third-grader who has dedicated her young life to the stage, would sing, and Maria, who could play point guard if it were that kind of wedding, would instead play the clarinet.

"Oh," I said, my voice catching. "That would be lovely."

What was I supposed to say? "No. Thanks, anyway. This isn't that kind of wedding, either." The woman happens to be one of my best friends.

Sensing the hesitation in my voice, Diana offered: "I have audition tapes."

Oh, yeah, sure. I'll listen to them and call her back and say, "Sorry, they aren't quite what I was looking for."

"Oh, don't be silly," I said instead.

Joe, the kid who hates chocolate, doesn't like "stuff" on his clothes, either. No logos, no decals, no pictures, no nothing. So I chose for him a white sweater over a blue oxford-cloth shirt and navy blue wool pants. You can't get any more plain than that.

He acknowledged the success of my purchases with a too, too cool, "Yeah. OK, Mom. Just tell me where to stand."

The apple never falls far from the tree.

Jessie looked like Pearl, Hester Prynne's daughter in "The Scarlet Letter." Unearthly, Puritan beauty with just a hint of devilment in her eyes.

Her hair was pulled back in two French braids that formed an auburn wreath around her head. Her dress, pale pinks in a bargello pattern with a stand-up antique lace collar, fell in scalloped layers to midcalf. When she spun on the tips of her Mary Janes, it rustled softly. And that was Jessie in the wedding pictures, spinning on her toes — a whirling pink cloud in front of the altar, during the most solemn prayers.

Amanda, my goddaughter, the child born just weeks before my own first child arrived, sang "Candle on the Water," and it was so perfectly, innocently beautiful that everyone in the tiny chapel cried. Maria had a new reed in her clarinet and every note of "Amazing Grace" was pure and clear. And she can dribble with both hands.

Joe, the rings in the pocket of his plain blue trousers, stood stock-still. But Jessie, holding her silk flowers and mine, peeked around and up at the face of her mother to see if there were tears.

Gary never let go of my hand, and his shook when he put the wedding band, wet with holy water, back on my finger. My voice caught during the "Prayer of the Couple" (edited slightly to reflect the facts): "God, you have blessed us with children. Help me to love and to nurture them and to step back when it is time for them to walk alone."

Gary's prayer asked for the strength to be a loving example of all the children could be.

Father Tom Burke said that Catholic marriage is the miracle of two becoming one — and it is especially miraculous that we still wanted to do it after 10 years.

My Irish Catholic mother-in-law beamed brighter than the flash on her camera. "I never pushed," she said as each guest offered her congratulations. But before it all began, too, too cool Joe asked his dad if he was nervous. "No, Joe. Not at all."

Were you nervous the first time, Joe asked.

"Yes," said Dad. "Real nervous. But I'm not nervous now, because I know how it all turns out."

# Chapter 2

# Like Mother, Like Daughter

# Trailed by a loving hologram

I HAVE HEARD women say that their mothers are their best friends, and I have wondered what they meant.

Do they stay up late with their mothers and give each other pedicures? Do they drink too much wine with their mothers and complain about their husbands, their children?

Are their mothers the ones they call when panic rises like a bubble inside their chests, when tears run down their faces, when nights go sleepless?

Are their mothers the ones they ask when they want an honest answer? Am I fat? Am I wrong?

What do women mean when they say their mothers are their best friends?

I don't know, because I have never thought of my mother as my best friend. I have plenty of buddies, many of whom have mothered me a time or two. But I only have one mother.

My mother and I have had plenty of lunches out, covered miles in malls, drunk too much, gossiped and told secrets. Like best friends. But she is still, and always will be, my mother.

I have been more conscious of that since I became a mother myself. And I have looked for her fingerprints on my own mothering. And that is what my mother's influences are, I think. Fingerprints. Not footprints. Small and light and hardly able to be seen.

I do not do many things because my mother did them. I do not do many things because she did not. But I find my sails are gently filled with puffs of wind that come from my mother, turning me ever so slightly in one direction or another. Not correcting my course — I am too proud to give her that much credit, I guess — but shifting it.

I am not a newspaperwoman because my mother, from my earliest memory, would buy the *New York Times* on Sunday and spend the week reading every page. But I am a newspaperwoman whose mother read the *Times*.

I did not postpone my own childbearing for a career because my mother did not bear me, her oldest, until she was 35. But I am the daughter of a woman who was secretary to one of the most powerful attorneys in Pittsburgh, and my first child was not born until I was 34.

Does my mother laugh at me because I am funny? Or am I funny because my mother has always laughed at me?

My mother had four daughters and no sons. So I am flying by the seat of my pants as I try to raise my own boy. But I never had ballet lessons, and my mother let me quit piano, so my own daughter has ballet lessons and I will not let her quit piano.

"This is not how the Kennedys behave at the table," I say at dinner. My mother said that, too.

But I have not lived my life in mimicry of my mother's life, just as I have not lived my life in reaction against hers. I like to think I have made my own choices, but I understand now that those choices have been informed by the choices my mother made even before I was born.

Without her life, my own would be as spare and simple, as two-dimensional as a child's drawing. She has provided the depth, the background music, the animation to my story.

My mother has never cast a menacing shadow over my life. She has stepped back so many times I am sure she has felt she cast no shadow at all. But I see her, like a hologram, from the strangest angles.

She has this odd, nervous habit of tapping her thumb on the tips of each finger, like playing some imaginary scales. I caught a glimpse of my mother when my 9-year-old daughter began to do the same with her fingers. We live in another city. She is not imitating her grandmother. It is what dancer Martha Graham called a "blood memory."

Who knows what other memories of my mother are coursing through my daughter's veins? Through mine? I wonder how they will show themselves.

My mother is aging now. Soon, before all her secret gifts to Jessie and me have revealed themselves, my mother will be only that — a memory. She will join my father in the next life, where I am sure he has a cup of coffee waiting for her on the stairs outside their bedroom door. He has always risen earlier than she.

That will leave me to be the grown-up. The mother. I do not fear her leaving me as much as I thought I might, because I keep finding her in the smallest details of my life. She does not invade my life or dominate it. She just colors it.

I know I will always see my mother everywhere.

Even in the tap, tap, tapping of my daughter's fingers.

# Work and home: Your worlds and welcome to them

MILLIONS OF LITTLE girls will go to work with their moms or their dads for "Take Our Daughters to Work Day," an event designed to boost the confidence of adolescent girls and expand their ambitions.

And everyone — except the little girls who get to skip a day of school — is angry.

Educators think the girls belong in the classroom, that this kind of consciousness-raising stuff should not interfere with a young girl's primary responsibility, which is to learn.

Mothers of sons want to know why the boys have been excluded. Don't they need to witness women working, too? The women who do not work outside the home feel slighted. Isn't their role a worthy option for girls?

And the Ms. Foundation, which organized this event three years ago, wants to know why young girls can't have one lousy day out of the year to call their own.

I am not sure one day, or 100 days, would ever be antidote enough to reverse the erosion of self-confidence I know is at work on my 9-year-old daughter.

A tour of my office and the sight of women in business suits is not going to persuade her to stop looking in the mirror and start thinking about all the things she can do with her life.

But I think the parties arguing over this event have missed the point.

I will bring Jessie to work with me and take her to lunch and tell her the world is her oyster.

But then I will take her home.

There I will show her the dishes in the sink and the unmade beds, and I will let her listen as I try to talk her brother through his latest dilemma, all the while trying to throw together a low-fat meal her father can microwave when he gets home late from work.

I will tell Jessie that this will also be her world. For whether she is a kindergarten teacher or an astronaut, a nurse or a heavy-equipment operator, she will probably also be a mother and a wife. A career, I will tell Jessie, is not something women do. As in, what do you do? It is something women also do.

The conservatives and the religious right are furious with the Ms. Foundation and the "feminist, careerist, anti-family" agenda they believe is promoted by "Take Our Daughters to Work Day."

They argue that this celebration devalues the role of women as linchpins in the home and sends girls the message that only work that is paid is valuable.

But the truth is, neither vision of a girl's future is accurate. I doubt that my daughter will ever make an irrevocable choice between career and family. She will probably do both. And she will probably do them at the same time.

I will tell Jessie how some of us choose to work and some choose to raise children, but many more of us don't get to make that choice.

I will tell her that women like me have the best of both worlds, but never feel that we belong in either.

I will tell her how torn we are. About how we feel that we are doing one thing too many and neither of them well. About how we envy the stay-at-home moms all the while fearing that they disapprove of us and suspect our disparagement of them.

I will talk about how proud our husbands are of our achievements and how grateful they are that we can share the financial burden, but how it is still true that they have one job and we have two.

I will tell her that although we talk cheerfully about the balance in our lives, what we really feel is that we are failing in two places instead of one.

The truth is, I will tell Jessie none of these things.

I would never want to extinguish the enthusiasm she has for her future, and my suspicion is that she will see these things for herself soon enough.

If she is to learn anything from "Take Our Daughters to Work Day," I want it to be that her options are limitless, and one of those options is to have children.

We should take our daughters to work and show them the women bankers, the women doctors, the women carpenters and the women engineers. And then we need to take them home and show them, not the unmade beds and the mountains of laundry perhaps, but, as best we can, the precious responsibility that they are to us and how much we love them and how earnestly we take the job of raising them.

Take your daughter to work. And then take her home. Show her both worlds. Because the odds are she will straddle those worlds one day.

# A blooming flower

RECITAL (N.) — FRENCH for "spending a bundle on a costume and driving your mother nuts for a week so you can be on stage for a minute and a half."

Can you tell? Jessie had her ballet recital (the third in her very young life), and we are both going to need therapy.

I have an unsightly rash on my forearm that the doctor says is "nerves," and 8-year-old Jessie now wants to have her hair pulled back in a bun and lacquered down every morning.

The top of her head feels like cardboard when she leaves for school, and I am afraid she is going to get brain damage from all the hair spray.

And we have another costume to hang in the closet. Though I am beyond sentimentalizing them (she did look adorable as a bluebird in "Hansel and Gretel" one year), I can't quite part with them.

I keep thinking she can use them to play dress-up. But that is a silly notion. The costumes are always ordered to fit in January, and by May it is like stuffing a sausage to get the girls into them.

And so this costume will take its place alongside the others, leaving plenty of room for the worn-once dresses that seem to fill a woman's life and closet: christening gown, first Holy Communion dress, flower girl dress, prom gown, bridesmaid's dress, wedding gown. And all the dresses you can never wear again after your first child is born.

I am not sure why it is so important to me that Jessie take ballet. I never did. And there are no dancing genes in her family history. I can't even walk in high heels, for heaven's sake.

And Jessie herself is ambivalent. She loves the dress-up part and she worships her teachers, Miss Sandy and Miss Leslie. But she is caught in an awkward space between robust athleticism and grace.

She can't decide whether she wants to swim the butterfly or dance like one. Her theater-pink tights have grass stains on the knees. Her slippers are so worn I swear she is wearing them when she skids her bike to a stop. Sometimes, I'm sure she is just in it for the blue eye shadow and the lipstick.

I'm in it for the flowers, I think.

When I was 5 or so, I was a bridesmaid in a Tom Thumb wedding pageant at our church. I'm not sure what the point of it was — kids all dressed up like members of a wedding party — but I still have the picture of me in my little gown and the memory of being incredibly special to my parents for one night.

And in my head, I still have the smell of the flowers that I carried. It was my first experience with carnations, and the smell was intoxicating. I stayed up late the night of the pageant, talked a blue streak to my parents while all my sisters slept, and inhaled again and again the fragrance of the tiny bouquet I would not put down.

Even now, the smell of carnations brings me a rush of that ancient excitement, a flutter of exhilaration just near the center of me. The feeling of being center stage and special.

So I knew the answer before Jessie asked, "Will I get flowers after we do our bow?"

That night, the auditorium was awash with flowers. There were more than 175 children in the recital, and I guess all their mothers must have been in Tom Thumb weddings. They carried for their daughters everything from single pink roses to heaping armfuls. The hot night air in the auditorium was thick with the moist, sweet smell of flowers.

Jessie was flawless — well, mostly flawless — during her $1^1/_2$ minutes as a Swiss doll. I almost did not recognize her — hair back off her pretty face, eyes wide and blue with shadow, lips a bright rosy color.

Afterward, I was frantic to find her in the crowd of tiny poodles, mice, cats, clowns and ballerinas. I saw her in the corner of the room where the children waited, changing from her slippers to her tennis shoes. I caught her looking at the mirror and pursing her lips.

The bouquet I had for her was no simple clutch of carnations. It was nearly as big as she, indicative, I think, of my daydreams for her.

I want Jessie to be brave and beautiful on the world's stage. I want her to know all the steps in life. I want her to be confident and fearless when so many eyes are upon her.

I want her to be able to walk in high heels.

And I want the scent of flowers to trigger in her the memory of being very special.

# The sweetest holiday

HALLOWEEN IS MY favorite holiday.

You don't have to buy a bunch of presents for people. You don't have to cook. And your mother doesn't call you and ask, with that familiar tone in her voice, "Well, are you coming home for Halloween this year?"

I have the fondest memories of Halloween from my childhood. My father would carve the pumpkin on Halloween night, scooping great gobs of pumpkin glop onto newspaper. Seems like I was a "bum" every year. My dad's old baggy clothes, candle black from the foil-covered pumpkin lid all over my face.

My sisters and I would just run wild in the dark, safe streets of our suburban cul-de-sac. Squealing with both fear and delight when we ran into friends hiding inside a costume. We felt so unshackled, so free of the constraints of homework, bath and bedtime. It was late and it was dark and we were loose!

My favorite treats were Clark Bars and Nestle Crunch. I saved those and gave the rest to my sisters. My school lunches were worth waiting for during all of November.

My clearest memory is of one family in the neighborhood who would always invite us in, so we saved their house for last. There would be a fire roaring in the fireplace, hot cider and powdered-sugar doughnuts. My mother would stay awhile and talk, and it was really late when we got home to bed. Like maybe 10 o'clock.

These days I do Halloween from a different angle, that of a parent.

We have gone to the same pumpkin farm every year since my oldest was born. Joe is not even a year old in the photo we have of him sitting in a pile of pumpkins there. Each child gets to choose a pumpkin. A tall, skinny one, a short, fat one. And then they pick a baby pumpkin for themselves. I buy the last of the season's tomatoes and some apple butter that grows old in my fridge. And my husband makes some wisecrack about the cornstalks that I want.

"Excuse me," Gary says. "You mean this stuff is sitting dead in a field somewhere and we are buying it? How are we supposed to get it home?"

Be glad I don't want to decorate with an old, rusty tractor, I tell him.

I make cupcakes for my children's classroom parties, and I take pictures of the costume parade at their school. (Their former principal would always wear a referee's uniform, complete with a whistle, and the parents would just howl with laughter.)

I am one of the lucky mothers. My husband does the costumes. (And the science fair and the dioramas and the classroom projects. Like the one of the amoeba that he and Joe did with bathroom caulk. Gary is the creative one. I'm the one who gets them where they need to be on time.)

He has made cardboard wings for Jessie the Angel and a cardboard suit of armor for Joe the Knight. He even made a whip for "Indiana Joe" one Halloween.

But the year that I labored into the night to put "jewels" around the neckline of Jessie's Indian princess costume, I was the hero. She was so happy she couldn't speak, she just hugged my legs. This year, of course, she has declared that she doesn't want to be a "dumb Indian princess."

Gary carves the pumpkin in the garage on Halloween night, scooping big globs of "pumpkin guts," as Joe calls it, onto newspaper. He makes the same joke every year: "Honey, do you want to save this for those homemade pies you make?" He sets himself up in the garage with a cup of coffee, talk radio, dim lights, a glowing pumpkin and a basket of candy.

I make my children eat something that resembles dinner. And I make them wait until it is officially dark. I go with them every step of their trick-or-treating way. I restrain the wild one and I hold the hand of the shy one. I want to put fluorescent tape on their costumes, but they howl their objections. I never let them go to a house if I don't know who lives there.

And when they finally go to sleep, I sort through their candy — or in Jessie's case, her candy wrappers — and try to squirrel some of it away to tuck into their lunches as a surprise. I only eat the Clark Bars or the Nestle Crunch.

On Halloween night, our house is everybody's last stop. We have a fire roaring in the fireplace. And while the parents sip hot cider and talk, the kids run wild and unrestrained through the nearby streets and backyards. It is late when everyone leaves. Maybe 10 p.m. And the powdered doughnuts are all gone.

# The crying games

NIKE HAS LAUNCHED a new advertising campaign, one that is chronicling the championship season of the Charleston Cougars, a fictional, high school girls basketball team.

In a series of 10 ads, Nike will introduce us to the players in vignettes that deal with one or another aspect of team sports:

Tryouts and the moment when you see your name on the team roster; the feeling of a brand-new uniform; the tortures of practice the day after you lose to a team you should have beaten; playing on the home court of last year's champions; hanging out in a hotel room when the team is on the road; the night when all your shots fall through the hoop.

"The ads are going for the universal experiences of sports," said Kathryn Reith, spokeswoman for Nike's women's sports division. "What it is like to be part of a team, whether you are on a high school girls' basketball team or a pro football team.

"It is about the experiences athletes share."

I asked Reith if there was crying.

"Crying?" she asked, a little confused.

Yes, I said. Crying. That's the shared experience of all the young female athletes I know.

I never played sports, so I can't speak from personal experience, I said. My husband played many sports, but all of them with his brothers and other boys.

But after careful observation of our daughter and her friends and teammates, we have concluded that crying must be the universal experience of girls in sports.

"There is no crying in basketball," exclaimed one soft-spoken dad/coach when one of his players burst into tears after his mildly impassioned instructions.

He was baffled, he told me, and I am sure he thinks he must hand out future coaching directions on flowered stationery.

Relationships are the meat and potatoes of girls' lives, and they don't leave them on the bench with their warm-up jackets and their water bottles.

It doesn't matter what kind of talent you have on the floor, if the girls are sulking or angry, the team will lose.

If they are feuding on the court, they will feud in real life. If they are feuding in real life, they will feud on the court.

A coach can't bench one player and start another in her place without first making an appointment for a group-therapy session.

If he yells at a player, he might as well remove her from the game, because she will be paralyzed by shame and self-doubt. And yet these same sensitive creatures can rip each other to shreds behind their backs.

The coach can't call for more passing, because the last one to take a shot will think he is talking about her, and she wouldn't shoot again if she were alone on the court.

He can't ask for better team rebounding because every player will think he is complaining about her rebounding.

And this appears to be true, not just at the recreational level, but at every level of girls sports.

"With men, coaching was a constant process of lancing overgrown egos," Anson Dorrance, head coach of the legendary University of North Carolina women's soccer team, once explained. "With women, it's a constant process of building egos up."

His dynasty has won 15 national championships in 17 years, and lost only four games in the last 296 it has played. He has coached the best women to ever play the game of soccer, and he says:

"I am constantly amazed by how little confidence even my most talented players have."

Dorrance's success can be explained by the tremendous players he recruits, his brutal conditioning program and his head for the game.

But the first building block in his program is "camaraderie." He convinces his players that they are playing not for North Carolina, not for a national crown, but for one another, for the players who have come before and the players who will come after.

In other words — relationships.

"If you have been involved in sports long enough, the sport itself loses its allure," Dorrance said before his team won this year's NCAA title. "But what I think always captivates you are the people you spend four years with.

"You want to do well by them."

Title IX was not enough. Girls sports are not just about money, scholarships, coaches, facilities and opportunities. All the money in the world can't buy a girl's freedom from the tyranny of her tender feelings, her need to please, her need to build relationships.

To succeed in sports, a girl must give in to the natural forces of competition and excellence and stop wondering if her teammates like her or if her coach is mad at her.

She must be what they say about the best men players: "He was unconscious."

The final installment in the Nike advertising series is called "The Championship," and you can guess the happy ending to the Charleston Cougars' season. It hasn't aired yet, of course, and I bet the girls will be crying.

That's the thing about girls' sports. After a big game, it is hard to tell the winners from the losers, because everybody is crying.

# My mother's handbag

MY MOTHER HAS been standing at the door with her handbag on her arm for a while now.

That has always been her signal, when visiting any of her four daughters, that it is time to go home.

She didn't really do that, of course — stand by the door with her handbag resting in the crook of her arm. But that is how we described the state of mild agitation she entered not very long after a visit began.

"You know Mother," we would say to each other in a tone of voice that sounded as if we were rolling our eyes. "Dinner isn't over 10 minutes and she is standing at the door with her handbag on her arm."

And then we would laugh at this vague homing instinct in our mother that kicked in when she was too long away from her house, from "her things," as she would say.

There is no house to return to now. And my mother's "things" have been reduced to a couple of bed pillows, a favorite bedspread and a few pieces of clothing that are easy to pull on and comfortable to wear.

She is visiting one of her daughters permanently now. She cannot stand by the door without a walker, and her handbag must be carried by one of her grandchildren.

My mother has settled into a life she promised herself and her daughters she would never live. A life lived with one of us.

"I know you will think I'm crazy," she says every now and again. "But I feel like I could get in my car and drive myself right home to old eighteen-eighty-two."

"You are crazy," we tell her. "You couldn't get the car door open."

My mother is angry at God, I think.

She has been standing at the door with her handbag over her arm for a while now, and he has ignored the signal that even her daughters recognized.

And now she feels she has overstayed her welcome. Her children are grown, they have married decent men and she doesn't need to worry any of them through any more pregnancies. "My job is done," she says, exasperated.

And still, God has not noticed her standing by the door.

My sister, Ellen, thinks God has other ideas. My mother laughs rue-fully that Ellen is stating the obvious, but Ellen is insistent that my mother's prolonged ill health is a blessing and a great gift to us all.

Four girls so caught up in their own family lives that they could eas-ily bury old angers and irritating differences have been required to come together and communicate in ways that have revealed the strengths of each to the other. And to the mother of us all.

My mother has seen the men her daughters married as working part-ners in busy and complicated family lives, not as lumps in her living room on a Sunday afternoon.

She has seen her daughters not as too busy for her — just too busy, overwhelmed as they are by overcommitted schedules.

Grandchildren who have been bored and boorish during visits to Grandma have been seen in their natural habitat. There they have shown themselves to be funny or hyper or thoughtful or troubled or pleasant or a struggle to raise.

My mother has seen her grandchildren for the holograms they are: different with each angle of light that hits them, not as the spoiled fruit of overindulgence.

And those children have seen the obligations each generation has to the previous one lived out in a vivid reckoning:

This is who we are. Daughters, sisters, mothers, wives. This, not a picnic on the Fourth of July, is the working definition of family.

This matrix of caring that we have constructed is holding together at the moment, but it is very fragile and we all know it. There is no priva-cy in this enterprise, no time to withdraw, no quiet place to which any of us can retreat. We live every moment of every day in obligation to my mother, and she lives every moment of every day with that knowledge.

"I thought I had planned for everything," says my mother, who made us all laugh when she organized and paid for her funeral while still a busy, healthy woman. "But I never planned for this."

This part of life is far more complicated than any of us ever imagined. My mother thought — we all thought, I guess — that all she would have to do is stand by the door with her handbag on her arm.

# Goodbye

JEAN KRAFT PETERSON Reimer took an uncommonly long time, for a woman of her generation, to get around to becoming my mother.

Born 80 years ago to a well-to-do and prominent family, she was the last of her siblings to marry, living at home with her widowed mother, working and playing the role of a sophisticated single girl until well into her 30s.

There are pictures of her in the family albums from the society columns of the newspapers and snapshots of her on the beaches of Conneaut Lake in Pennsylvania, a scandal in her two-piece bathing suit, a cigarette between long fingers with long red fingernails, bangle bracelets cascading almost to her elbow.

She was the fourth of six children and a twin, but it was her younger sister, Elizabeth, with whom she was closest. The two were such a tumble of laughter and good times that the family nicknamed them Brenda and Cobina, after a pair of '40s "celebutantes" who dominated the gossip columns of the day. The nicknames stuck so well that I grew up thinking that "Jean" was short for "Cobina" and Aunt Betty's full name was "Brenda."

When my mother was not traveling with her friends to the beaches of Conneaut or New Jersey or attending dances at the country clubs that dot Western Pennsylvania, she worked as a legal secretary to one of the most powerful lawyers in Pittsburgh, playing the role of Della Street before there was a "Perry Mason Show."

She dressed in the most sophisticated clothes and always wore white gloves to work. Her handbag matched her shoes, and she never would have dreamed of trotting to work with socks and tennis shoes pulled over her hose or of carrying a giant canvas tote. Years later, when she worked in downtown Pittsburgh with three of her daughters, she would continue to set that standard for us.

In Jean's day, legal secretaries were the confidantes and trusted assistants of the lawyers for whom they worked. Jean followed her boss into court and took notes, handled his personal checkbook, bought gifts for him to give to friends and family, and kept his social calendar. She was indispensable.

It was during this time that Jean met a handsome and wealthy bachelor who, unfortunately for my sisters and me, was not to be our father.

A jet-setter in the infancy of airplanes, he was stuck in Hawaii, where he owned land and businesses, during a strike against TWA. During the prolonged absence of the man who had given her a cocktail ring studded with 20 diamonds, my mother met my father, an athletic and dashing farm boy from New Kensington, Pa., who charmed his way into her country clubs even though he didn't have the change in his pocket to tip the locker-room attendant.

They met at a country club dance in August, and my mother bought him four new tires so he could court her. In March, they married in a candlelight evening church service. My mother wore a tea-length dress that was the height of fashion.

My father's mother, the imperious Jenny Reimer, known to the family as Aunt Jane, so disapproved of the sophisticated city girl who had snared her oldest son and her support in widowhood that she refused to come down from her bedroom for the wedding until after my father went in, closed the door and spoke to her.

Mother said she never asked what passed between them, but Aunt Jane made it to the church on time. It was not until June a year later, when the first child was born, that Aunt Jane's heart melted toward my mother.

Jean spent the first year of my life trapped and unhappy in a tiny set of rooms in New Kensington, Pa. The role of wife and mother was a far cry from the life she had known in the courthouses of Pittsburgh and the country clubs of Western Pennsylvania.

But 14 months later, there was Cynthia, affectionately referred to as "Junior" in my father's letters to my mother — he would never get a son. Ellen and Elizabeth Jean, whose name combined those of the inseparable sisters, followed quickly. My mother had three toddlers and an infant as she entered her 40s.

She also had a husband who traveled for Alcoa and returned home only every other weekend, no car, a paycheck just once a month, a wringer-washer, no dryer and a mountain of cloth diapers. There were no malls, no McDonald's, no baby-sitters, no preschool. No kindergarten, even, for she did not have the $5 monthly bus fare.

What she did have was a wonderful set of friends in a suburban cul-de-sac. Like so many neighborhoods of the late 1950s and early 1960s, it sprang up to support the emerging junior executive population of corporate America. The years my family spent in that cocoon of sameness, with a hundred children our age and their mothers my mother's friends, were the happiest of our lives.

My sisters and I drove away our mother in the regrettable but inevitable rebelliousness of adolescence and the conceit of young adulthood. It is only now, I think, that we, each of us, regret that wasted time. She was always funny and interesting and good company, but we were too aloof then to include her in our lives.

When we had husbands and children of our own, that gap was bridged with a sharp understanding of what her life had been like and a deep appreciation for the woman she had become. We never let our mother be our mother again — we had grown too far away for that, and our chaotic family lives were a mystery to her — but we allowed her to be a companion, an adviser, a confidante, a friend.

It is that friend, and that friendship, we mourn now.

My mother, the gay and elegant Cobina, the last of a lively brood of six, died Aug. 20. It had been Brenda's birthday.

# Chapter 3

# *My own personal* Cavemen

# Back in the cave, pal

I WENT TO see Rob Becker's one-man show "Defending the Caveman" and left thinking that my husband should put Becker on retainer. No man is more in need of defending right now than my own personal caveman.

That's because he and I had a date for that show and he stood me up. Scheduled an out-of-town business trip. On our anniversary.

Is he Rob Becker's poster boy or what?

I planned this evening of fine dining and theater — women are always doing the planning — because I felt like 14 years of marriage in the current national rush to divorce merits more celebration than saloon food and a movie at the local multi-plex cinema.

Because my own personal caveman is not fond of live theater unless the actors are wearing uniforms and concentrating on some sort of ball, I thought this would be the perfect compromise.

Rob Becker in jeans and a T-shirt marching back and forth across the stage at the Lyric Opera House announcing that men are not idiots is just the ticket for the man who refers to intermission as "halftime" and who, after a performance of "Miss Saigon," said he thought there should have been more about the war.

Anyway, I purchased four tickets so that my own personal caveman would have the commiseration of his longtime friend, Steve, and I would have the company of Steve's wife, Diana.

Steve and Gary have been friends since college, when they were regularly unsuccessful with women together. Diana and I brought them into the world of love and family, but we have often felt more like we came between them.

But we agreed that these two friends would certainly enjoy hearing, for two hours, that we were wrong in all our harsh judgments of them. We also felt that they might gain some insight into why it is they are so often in trouble with us. They agreed to go so they would not be in trouble with us, and Diana and I said this was a good start.

Well, I remember the day I married this man like it was yesterday, but it appears he would have trouble remembering it even if it was yesterday. Marking things down on a calendar has always worked for me, but that requires a calendar and my husband doesn't have one, so he double-booked himself into a trip to Wisconsin to research a story about ice-fishing.

Fall in, I said when he told me.

As you might imagine, Steve's commitment to the evening's entertainment disappeared like chips during a football game, to use one of Becker's favorite themes. So I gathered a car full of women and off we went to hear a defense of the very behavior we had just witnessed.

In one of the great juxtapositions of all time, my own personal caveman was spearing sturgeon through a hole in the ice about the same time I was getting dressed to the nines for an evening of theater. Exhibit A in defense of the caveman. I only wish Becker had taken questions from the audience.

But, as we learned from the O.J. Simpson trial, every accused is entitled to the best defense money can buy, and Becker's explanation of how a man's mind works was worth every penny. I learned that men are not wrong, they are just different, and it is a shame my own personal caveman was not there to witness my epiphany because now I can deny it whenever it suits me and more's the pity for him.

My own personal caveman returned from his business trip last night and I am sure he believes that the hurt feelings that resulted from his scheduling misstep have passed and all will be well when he comes down to breakfast this morning.

And opens this newspaper.

# One man's trash

HE WAS CLEANING out his closet. . . . Poor choice of words. He was moving things around in his closet. Nothing ever actually made its way out.

Anyway, my husband was moving things around in his closet, making space for more things that he was not throwing away, when he said: "You know, I have stuff made by companies that don't exist anymore."

He paused and considered.

"You know, I have stuff made in countries that don't exist anymore."

What a revelation! Would this be the moment that he realized he was carrying way too much baggage in life? That he needed to lighten his load? Doubt it.

They say women are sentimental collectors. That their attics are crammed with baby clothes and handmade Mother's Day cards and letters from dear friends. That bulk trash pickup day is not scheduled with women in mind. That it is men who carry old boat engines and boxes of plywood to the curb.

Not in my house. Not my husband. It is I, and just about any woman I know, who sorts and sorts and throws out.

"During the day when they are all gone, I go through the house and collect their junk," my sister says. "I throw it out or take it to Goodwill. Then I deny it at the dinner table."

Her husband works on barges on the river, and he buys his work clothes from Goodwill. She's so afraid he is going to go shopping one day and actually buy his old clothes back.

A neighbor fellow was a charter subscriber to *National Review* in 1963, and he has kept every single copy for more than 30 years. Why? I ask.

"After 30 years, I don't need a reason," he says.

"And," he adds, "if I were to discontinue doing it, my wife might have reason to worry about the security of her position. I know she was tiptoeing around when I got rid of the car I'd had for 18 years."

Well she might. They've only been married 16 years. The magazines and the car had more seniority than she.

Another friend's husband seems quite incapable of parting with his old running shoes. Instead, he just assigns them a new job description. All 12 pairs.

"There are the racing running shoes and the daily workout running shoes," she says, "and the ceremonial running shoes and the coaching-baseball running shoes, the grass-cutting running shoes and the patio-party running shoes."

The husband of another friend has 40 ball caps. My sister's husband has 165 T-shirts from road races. "We added a third floor to this house because he can't throw anything away," she says.

A Sunfish sailboat had been sitting under our deck since we moved in. Ten years. The mast had rotted and the sails had disintegrated, but the fiberglass hull was in great shape and a neighbor offered us $600 for it. No sale.

My husband had never sailed the single-handed boat on the raging Chesapeake Bay. It was a relic from his bachelor life in Western Pennsylvania and a man-made lake so shallow that you could stand on its cement-covered bottom if you capsized. This is a very cautious guy.

"Rosebud," was all he said when I asked why he would not sell. When you ask them why, they always have good reasons:

"I might make something out of it."

"I'm going to wear it when I lose weight."

"I'm going to fix it."

"It's still in good shape."

"It's going to be worth something someday," is the reason a friend heard when she told her husband that it was time he threw out the sports magazines he's been saving since the 1950s.

"Everyone in the free world knows the value except me, I guess," she says. "I told him that since we were moving and could use the extra money, it would be a perfect time to sell.

"He looked like an animal caught in my headlights, absolutely haunted. He mumbled something about how it wasn't the right time to sell."

Such separation anxieties. My husband was so morose the day before bulk trash pickup, as he wheeled the old lawn mower ("I was going to fix it") to the curb at my command. But when he returned to add the gas-tank cap, the mower was gone. Bulk trash scavengers had taken the mower in the blink of his eye.

He realized that other men were throwing out their perfectly good junk, too. That night, late, he came to me wearing an old jacket ("It's still in good shape") and a ball cap pulled down over his eyes. "I'm going out there," he announced, setting his jaw. "There is great stuff out there."

# Mouthing off

"WE DON'T TALK anymore."

Bet you thought that was me speaking. Another woman whining about the quality of marriage to a man who reads the paper during meals and watches TV the rest of the time.

Well, you would be wrong.

My husband, who often begins the day by opening the newspaper and then saying, "Your boy Clinton has done it again," doesn't feel like I am holding up my end of the marriage, conversation-wise.

He is right, sad to say. At the end of the day, I just don't have it in me for much more than, "uh-huh."

It wasn't always this way. I used to be his conversational equal.

As probably the only husband and wife pro football writers in the country, we could talk NFL business until the final gun sounded.

How many women do you know who can explain why small, quick linemen are so important to a trap-blocking offense? Or who can handicap a playoff game without so much as a press guide in her hand? My husband didn't know how good he had it.

Then we had kids.

When they were young and I was starved for intelligent conversation after a day of burbles and cooing, I found the energy to talk sports — plus politics, the economy, neighborhood crime, international affairs or gossip about the stars — when their father came home.

With a newborn at the breast and a toddler on the hip, my body ached badly at the end of the day. But I could still talk.

That has changed. Now at the end of the day, I have no energy to answer my husband, the human op-ed page. Now, it is my brain that aches like an overworked muscle. I am all talked out.

"How do you get to be homeless?" "How can a baseball player make more money than the president?" "Can you have a baby without being married?" "Can a burglar get up to our bedrooms if he uses a gun to shoot out the alarm?" "Why didn't our army just find Saddam Hussein and kill him?"

My two children pepper me with questions all day long. Some are pretty heavy, and mine will be the first words they hear on these subjects.

And so I measure my words with care. Each response should be worthy of being stitched onto a sampler, I tell myself. I try to answer them with some combination of the real and the ideal. Little glimpses of how the world really works, shaded with hopes for how it should work.

I admit, most of their questions don't deserve such a civilized answer: "Why can't we watch 'Married With Children'?" "Why can't we go to the pool now?" "Why can't we go to Chuck E. Cheese?"

"Because I say so," will do nicely on those occasions. "I don't want to hear about it" is another of my favorites, along with "Not now, I'm on the phone."

My job description has changed as my children have grown older. I no longer am responsible for simply feeding them and making sure neither one falls down the steps. I spend my day helping them form their values, their view of the world, their feelings about themselves. It is the toughest talking we grown-ups ever do.

And it is not always convenient. They rarely ask this stuff during a quiet moment in front of the fire. They come to you with their earnest questions across the floor you just mopped. Or they wait until bedtime, when you are at your lowest ebb, to start a conversation worthy of a Harvard Divinity School roundtable.

Of course, some of my work is not so high-minded. "Because no one wants to hear you burp." "Save that bathroom talk for your friends." "We do not eat while standing up. I want both cheeks on the chair until you are done." "When a grown-up says something to you, you should at least look at them."

Raising children is a constant process of civilizing them. They are born with an innate sense of fairness, but they are not born with an innate sense of manners. It has become clear to me that you have to teach them every single one. And if your children don't attend Gilman School, where civility is currently on the curriculum, you have to do it yourself.

And so forgive me, husband, if at the end of the day, all I can do is read the newspaper or stare numbly at a television.

The poor, neglected man has had a vision of how this will play out.

"You'll become a famous columnist and then you will get your own radio talk show," he predicted. "One day, you'll say, 'Let's go to Gary in Annapolis,' and it will be me, calling to talk about Bosnia."

# Stripping away Mom's rules

HAVE YOU EVER noticed that no matter how late you call home or return home, when you have left the children in the care of their father, they are still not in bed?

Have you ever felt that you might stay out all night, return home at dawn and find the kids still awake?

So, as you might guess, I was not surprised to call home from work one night at 10:30 and hear the sweet voices of my children in the background.

"What are the kids doing still awake?" I asked.

"We're playing strip poker," was my husband's response.

(Long, uncomfortable pause here.)

"They didn't want to get undressed for bed," he said, "so I told them we were going to play strip poker and when they got down to their underwear they had to go to bed.

"Jessie came to the table in an overcoat and with shoes and socks on. She said she didn't think she would play very well."

Have you also noticed that when dad is in charge, the rules are different?

According to a study of census figures done by the Population Reference Bureau and released last week, fathers are the primary caregivers for 20 percent of the children in this country under age 5.

What the study did not show, however, is that fathers seem to have a lot more trouble in the areas of bedtime ("They didn't want to go"), clothing ("That's what she wanted to wear"), meals ("It was easier to go out") and social propriety ("That's the movie they wanted to rent") than mothers ever do.

One father I know sent his daughter to school in a nightgown because it looked like a dress. Another sent his little girl out the door wearing her petticoat on top of her dress so, as she demanded, the ruffles would show.

One father spends a precious morning hour with his preschoolers, who will be asleep when he returns from work, taking them out for Slurpees and bubble gum that has a free tattoo in it. Another takes his children to the pool every summer night his wife is away because it is easier than bathing them.

Still another father tells his 4-year-old son to be sure to pack a napkin in his lunch, and then fails to notice that it is a sanitary napkin. (The child could read, just not that well.)

It is clear that men don't share the standards we relentless mothers have established. I rent "My Fair Lady" and "West Side Story" to watch with my children. I talk about the origin of musical theater and the themes of race and class prejudice. My husband rents "Spaceballs," and he and the kids curl up under an afghan and laugh like crazy.

I sign them up for art classes. He sits at the kitchen table and draws whatever it is they want to color — a jet plane, a basket of flowers, a cobra, a kitten.

Most modern fathers have been on the scene since the delivery room. We have asked that they be equal partners in parenting, that they do more than simply take the casserole out of the oven when mom is at card club.

They don't have the excuses our fathers had when things fell apart without mom around. They don't get to play dumb. They have to know that the amoxicillin is found in the fridge and not the medicine cabinet — details that may have escaped fathers in the Robert Young mold, who simply came home at 6 p.m., slipped on the sweater with the elbow patches and snapped open the evening paper.

And modern fathers have the added burden of living up to the standards of us control-freak, professional mothers. We are more than willing to let dad share in the trials and triumphs of raising children — as long as they do it our way. Our relentless criticism and niggling judgments can't make for a very pleasant environment in which to parent — a trial-and-error proposition if ever there was one.

That charitable concession made, let me also say that I have never been among three or more women where fathering foibles have not been discussed in a kind of "I-can-top-that" manner.

But the men whom I have ridiculed here are the same men who take their children crabbing, coach them in sports, volunteer in their school library, build models with them, do flash cards with them and snuggle with them until they fall asleep.

And so, on the night when my children and their father played strip poker, I simply said, "OK. But when they want to play 'dress poker' in the morning, you have to deal with it."

# Birth blues

HOUSTON OILER DAVID Williams missed his team's game in New England because he decided to stay with his wife for the birth of their first child — and for a while afterward. And it cost him a game check worth $125,000.

The outrage of his boss, offensive line coach Bob Young, who compared the game with World War II and said Williams' absence for such a sentimental reason was as unacceptable as it would have been during the war, was met with equal outrage by Houston fans and talk-show callers, some of whom offered to contribute money to help Williams make up the lost paycheck.

The Oilers' management was quick to point out that the child, Scot Cooper Williams, arrived at 6:25 p.m. CDT Saturday and that Williams had 17 1/2 hours to make it to Foxboro Stadium for the game against the New England Patriots.

They also said emphatically that they never asked Williams to make a choice between witnessing the birth of his first child or playing in the football game. He simply should have hustled to make a late plane, the team said.

I don't know. If I'm Mrs. David Williams, I take the $125,000.

Ask around. Was the presence of the husband during the labor and delivery of the child worth a week's pay? Maybe. Maybe not.

Maybe you are married to a husband like mine. Great guy, great father. All that. But not exactly indispensable in the birthing suite.

I'm lying there like I'm in shock because I'm delivering a month early and the baby has not turned and it has to be an emergency Caesarean section and my husband, dressed now in hospital scrubs to accompany me, is looking at himself in the mirror and saying, regretfully, "A 'C' in organic chemistry and this could have been me. I could have been a doctor."

What a tower of strength.

Talk to any woman — and then talk to her husband — about the wonder of their partnership during the glorious birth of their children, and it sounds as if they weren't even in the same room.

"I was in the middle of a trial, and I called the court and told them I wouldn't be in," said a lawyer friend. "Being a father is more than conceiving the child. You have to be there for the start, and you have to follow it through."

Now listen to his wife. "I started labor at midnight and woke him up. He was hungry, so he asked if I could hold off until he got some Chinese food."

He says: "If I hadn't been there, we would have had a problem. Thanks to the Lamaze classes, I knew when she was ready to go. I had to practically fight with the hospital staff about it. Finally, they checked her, and I had been right."

She says: "He's down the hall eating pretzels with the nurses and my water breaks. I'm shrieking for him or for a nurse or for anybody. Finally, he comes in, breathing pretzel breath all over me, saying, 'Honey, what's the problem?' "

He says: "She had back labor. It was really painful for her, so I spend the whole time rubbing her back. She got pretty irritable. A husband might be the only person who would put up with that."

She says: "He wanted out. Four hours of labor was beyond his attention span. I just decided then and there that any more kids and it was going to be a real short labor."

He says: "Williams' coach is a Neanderthal. 'Let me know if it comes out all right' is an archaic view. There are certain things that only happen once. There may be other children, but this child will only be born once."

She says: "With my daughter, it looked like false labor, but they kept me all night to make sure. That meant my husband had to sleep in a chair if he was going to stay. Every 15 minutes, he says, 'So, honey, do you want me to stay?' "

To be serious, husbands must be there for the birth of their children for more than sentimental reasons. If there is something wrong with that child or if the child does not live, the tragedy is too much to be borne by the woman alone. It must be borne by both; that is part of the marriage contract. No job can supersede that.

And so I needed and wanted my husband, the Dr. Welby wanna-be. I couldn't have made it without him. He was there for me when the spinal block failed and the Caesarean birth produced tremendous pain.

He was there beside me when I reached for his hand, and then his throat and said, my voice a groan: "I want furniture and jewelry for this."

# Go figure: This is a sport, OK?

REAL MEN DON'T like figure skating. Just ask the real man who controls the remote control in your life. He'll tell you it is not a sport.

It is not a sport if you wear sequins when you do it. It is not a sport if the music they play while you do it matters. It is not a sport if you do it while holding a woman in your arms. And it is not a sport if people watching decide who wins.

But the men of America will be good sports this month when women seize control of the television to watch the Winter Olympics from Lillehammer, Norway. Women love figure skating, and CBS will make sure there is plenty to watch.

Figure skating produced among the all-time highest-rated sports broadcasts during the 1992 Albertville Winter Games, and CBS will load its prime-time shows with skating during the 10 nights of competition. By some estimates, figure skating will make up 60 percent of the total Olympic package.

CBS expects a viewing audience of better than 185 million Americans, and 55 percent of them will be women -- upper-income, highly educated women. "Figure skating is what brings them in," says George Schweitzer, senior vice president for marketing. "It has all the glamour women like."

A recent survey of readers by *USA Today* only confirmed this. Women respondents overwhelmingly described themselves as "die-hard" Olympics fans. And 65 percent of them said their favorite sport was figure skating. Only 8 percent of the men agreed.

The men surveyed said their favorite sports were Alpine skiing and hockey. Hey, what a surprise.

Men view figure skating as an art form, like modern dance or ballet, something you attend when your wife makes you and while wearing a jacket and tie. It is only a sport if you bleed or get dirty doing it or if you can drink beer while watching it. It takes a flurry of accusations that one woman skater called in a hit on another to get the men of America interested.

In my previous life as a sportswriter, I covered figure skating — lots of it. And it was plenty sport enough for me.

I admit, my stories read more like a combination wedding announcement-theater review ("She wore a crimson frock, beads glistening on the tight-fitting bodice. The music cast a spell broken only by thunderous ovation." That kind of thing.)

And I know it was unprofessional of me to cry when Brian Boitano skated to "The Music of the Night," but, my God, there was just so much emotion, so much lyrical sadness in his performance. . . . Sorry. I still get carried away.

Anyway, as I said to my husband, the pro football writer, I'd like to see the Washington Redskins' Darrell Green — for years "the fastest man in the National Football League" — move as fast as Boitano does, stop on a dime, jump and spin three times in the air and then land on one foot — one blade, actually.

In my book, that's a sport.

My husband was forced to admit that figure skating fits his criteria for a sport. "If you have to wear special shoes, it is a sport," he says. (Swimming qualifies, he says, because if you wore flippers, you would be better at it.)

I came to appreciate the consuming dedication and the killer instincts that lay behind the sequins and silk when the U.S. Figure Skating Championships were held in Baltimore in 1989, the year that eventual Olympic gold medalist Kristi Yamaguchi burst on the scene.

After a week of competition, the championships closed with an exhibition. The winners, liberated from the stifling requirements of judges and the driving need to win, let it all hang out.

I decided to take my son, who had just started taking ice-skating lessons, to see this last festive performance. My husband was immediately suspicious. He took Joseph on his knee and said, "Son, when you get home, Daddy is going to tell you all about Gordie Howe."

So guys, be patient while your women watch, transfixed, as the Olympic figure skating competition unfolds. Never mind how they drift with the music and weep at the stories the skaters tell on the ice. Take a nap, get a beer, or think of my poor husband.

For months before he left to cover the Olympics, he collected expensive Arctic gear and daydreamed of covering real men in real sports, like Norwegian cross country skier Vegard Ulvang, who actually crossed Greenland on skis.

All of that, only to find out that his assignment was to cover figure skating.

# Growing pains

THIS WILL BE the summer of Joe's 10th year, the summer of letting go.

I can see in my son an anxiousness to be free of little boydom. In me, there is just anxiousness about the little freedoms that I will be forced to grant, about the freedoms he will stretch and embroider, about rules he will bend and break, just to see if I am serious, just to see how far he can get.

I have seen it coming all this year. He pressed me to be allowed to return to the school playground with his buddies, and came home with new words to try out on me. I could see him calculate my reaction. Just what do mothers do when you say those things? On another trip to that playground, he was threatened by some older boys and tried not to show how shaken it had left him. He is ready for all this. I'm not so sure about me.

My own memories come into focus about the age of 10, so I am conscious of this turning point for him. It pains me to think that all we have done together up to now will be lost to him, that it will be me telling him about the memories, not him remembering them. That what has meant the most to me during these 10 years will exist only in photo albums for him.

But I am also pleased with the kind of clean slate his amnesia will give me. We can start over, sort of, building this wonderful relationship that will sustain us through his adolescence.

I'm not sure how to do it, though. I had sisters. I don't know what it is like to be a 10-year-old boy.

At 10, I was waiting to wear a bra and shave my legs. He wants to ride his bike across a four-lane road to play at a dock on a deep and forbidding stream.

I was trying to get my mother to let me have bangs. He wants to spend all day in the woods where liquor bottles have been found and where teen-agers smoke. I don't know if I will like it if I can't hear his voice through the screen door.

While I wanted to read "Archie and Veronica" comic books and drink

Cokes with older girls when I was 10, Joe has buddies with Swiss army knives and real bows and arrows.

My girlfriends' mothers took me with them to the new mall in our neighborhood. Joe has a friend whose dad might take him hunting. Did I think he was going to play Legos in front of the television for the rest of his life?

Joe and his dad are best friends now. It used to be me. Now, I feel like a woman who comes in to do the wash. But why would you want to go to a children's theater performance of "Cinderella" when somebody else will take you to the batting cages? So soon? He used to love seeing plays with me.

Now, he and his dad trade their mild bathroom jokes in whispers out of earshot of disapproving me. When Joe fidgets in church, it is his dad who settles him by telling him to pray for hits.

His father is now endlessly amusing while I — his partner during years of intimate moments — have become a bore. "Ohhhh, mom!" is what I hear most often these days.

Joe used to wear the polo shirts, khakis and Docksiders I chose for him. (His father says I dressed him like someone I would like to have dated.) Now, most days, he looks like a pile of dirty wash — and glad of it. His long, delicate fingers are always filthy now — I swear, it looks as if he digs for his food — and his nails are chipped and broken. He still slips that little paw into my hand when we walk, but I wonder how long that will last.

He doesn't seem to be very curious about sex. I guess I am grateful for that. But there is one girl in his class that he doesn't absolutely hate, and he endures endless teasing when he refuses to disparage her.

He never cared if his teeth were brushed, but suddenly he cares what his hair looks like. Oh my, I can see him in a prom tux! I don't like what he chooses to wear to school; I will never approve of whom he wants to date.

How did we get to this point, Joe and I? How did I, a college hippie and a ground-zero feminist, end up with a station wagon full of Little Leaguers? How did I, who wanted the sports section of my college newspaper disbanded as irrelevant, come to feel such pride in the fact that my son bats second and fields like Chris Sabo?

Joe and I got to this point together, I guess, traveling down the same road these 10 years. I can't help but wonder when that road will fork for us. Sometime in the next 10 years, I suppose.

# Are you ready for some football?

THIS SUNDAY IS Super Bowl Sunday, a kind of unofficial national holiday. Americans gather around the television set, eat too much, drink too much and cheer for football teams they never cared about before.

It has long been a cause for celebration in my house, too, but for a different reason. For 11 years, Super Bowl Sunday meant the end of the pro football season for my husband, the pro football writer.

He would leave home and hearth around July 15, when football training camps open, and travel every weekend and many Monday nights to exotic places such as Cleveland, Buffalo and Pittsburgh. He called it the "Kielbasa Triangle."

Integrating a family life with the pro football season was not easy. We might be the only couple who ever planned the birth of a child to occur between the Super Bowl in January and the start of the now-defunct United States Football League season in late February. I would pray for Washington to make playoffs only because that meant a week or two more of my husband in town.

Too many Thanksgivings were spent in Dallas or Detroit, where Thanksgiving Day football games have long been a tradition. Christmas was something we did very quickly between the end of the regular season and the start of the playoffs. My husband spent most New Year's Eves in a Hyatt Regency in some playoff town or another.

Covering the NFL might be the most prestigious job in sports, and so my husband was a hero to all his male friends, who asked wistfully what it was like. "It is like sex," my husband would say. "When you get paid for doing it, it changes the nature of the whole experience."

To my friends, I was an object of pity. The ultimate football widow. They would all look out for me, especially during the month of January, when I seemed particularly vulnerable. The Super Bowl is so close, I would tell myself. Just hang on.

One year, I very nearly did not.

It was January 1987, and the New York Giants were playing the Denver Broncos in the Rose Bowl in Pasadena. And it was snowing like crazy in Maryland.

Joe was not yet 3 years old, and Jessie was not yet a year old. My husband packed his shorts and left for California, and bad things started to happen to me almost immediately.

A blizzard arrived with a driving wind that actually pushed snow through the vents in our roof. I had snow drifts in my attic, and as they melted, they turned my bedroom ceiling into mashed potatoes. Plaster dropped in great dollops on the quilt on my bed.

On the way to the grocery store, I slid on the ice and wrecked the car. Inside the grocery store, my wallet was stolen. On the way home, I learned from the bank that I could get no more money. The Internal Revenue Service, impatient for me to pay a bill it had sent to an address I had vacated five years before, had attached my wages.

I had no food, no money, no car, two babies and a hole in my bedroom ceiling.

And my husband called. It was the Saturday before the big game, and all his work was done. For the first time that week, he checked on his little family in Annapolis.

The dam broke and I wailed. The car. My wallet. The roof. The IRS.

"Calm down," Gary said, "or something bad might happen."

"LIKE WHAT?" I asked, shrieking now.

"Wait a minute," I said. "Your voice sounds funny. Where are you calling from?"

"A pay phone," he answered, and his voice now sounded nervous, too.

"Why a pay phone? Where are you anyway?" I demanded.

There was an awkward silence on the phone line from California. "Disneyland," he mumbled.

"OH, YEAH? In more ways than one," I said before slamming down the phone.

On the flight home, the other sportswriters gathered around my husband with their notebooks open as he carefully recounted my Super Bowl week. When their own snowbound wives tried to punish them for a week in the sun, they simply offered up my miserable experiences.

"You think you had it bad? Listen to what happened to Gary's wife..."

After a dozen years, my husband has left pro football and now covers the Olympics. He's been around during this NFL season, but he will spend three weeks in February in Lillehammer. I'm trying to stay cheerful.

At least, I tell myself, it is cold in Norway and there is no Disneyland.

# Friendship in the shallow end

MY HUSBAND HAS a best friend, and they've been best friends for 30 years. But his wife and I like to say that we could empty the house into a moving van, pack up the kids, clean out the bank accounts and tack a goodbye note to the front door with a steak knife — and it would not come up in their conversations.

Now my husband's best friend is suffering with a bad back. He is confined to bed. He is heavily medicated. And he is depressed, quite reasonably, at the prospect of back surgery.

My husband rushed to the side of his friend to deliver the kind of comfort only one man can give another.

He watched an NBA game with him.

I am not making a judgment here — these two men have stayed close over many miles and many years, and their relationship is a model — but men and women go about the business of friendship quite differently.

If it were a woman friend of mine who was down with a bad back, I'd have organized everyone we know into wave after wave of meals and car pools.

We'd have divided her responsibilities into bite-sized pieces and then swallowed them up into our daily routines so that her life would continue seamlessly until she recovered.

But I doubt any of us would sit still long enough to watch TV with her.

This would be the stuff of 5 o'clock, wine-on-the-porch conversation among my women friends and me — except that we all have sons. And one of the things parents must teach their children, along with how to ride a two-wheeler and how to cut their own meat, is how to be a friend.

Because mothers seem to bear the burden of this kind of quality-of-life instruction, it falls to us. And because men and women are such different kinds of friends, we are as ill-equipped to teach our sons this as we are to teach them how to throw a curveball.

"I thought I could reach him about how to be a friend," says a friend, speaking of her son. "But he is 11 now, and he is slipping away and becoming his father."

Just when we think our sons are mature enough to understand friendship, trust and compassion, they have metamorphosed into buddies or teammates, distancing themselves from each other in some junior version of homophobia.

Put my daughter in a room with two 9-year-olds she has never met, and, within minutes, they will have formed a club, made a list of names and jobs in the club and started a newsletter.

But when I tried to convey to my son the pain of a boy in his class who was feeling excluded and isolated, he looked at me as though he was waiting for me to get to the point. "Yeah? And?"

At the beach in the summer, my daughter introduces each new friend with lengthy biographical notes. "This is Nicole. She lives on a farm in Pennsylvania and they have 300 cows and her dad has to get up very early in the morning and their grandmother lives with them."

But my 11-year-old son will play all day in the sand with a strange boy, and they will not even exchange names. Jessie will want her new friend to come to dinner and spend the night. Joe and his buddy will part without a word.

In boys or men, there does not seem to be the emotional exchange that characterizes women's friendships. No intimacy, no confiding, no sharing of weaknesses.

"Why do we discount it because it is not like ours?" asks a friend who is raising three sons. "Because it wouldn't satisfy us, is it wrong?"

Perhaps not. But what comfort does that give a mother who watches helplessly as her son moves awkwardly in and out of friendships? Just because there is no depth does not mean there is no pain. It is not only a little girl who will cry because someone's loyalties have shifted. What language do we use to console our boys when they have been dismissed as a friend? How do we teach them not to be that kind of a friend?

All of this is only important if social scientists are right and there would be less violence in the world if men could unburden themselves in friendship the way women do, if men could relate in some way other than the competitive dynamics of sports or business.

Perhaps men's friendships are not substandard; perhaps they are just different. Men may not be confiding and empathetic, but they are loyal and they are available.

And when your back goes out, they sit with you and watch the NBA on TV.

# Bigger than both of us

WHEN I SAW my nephew Rudi dressed in uniform for his junior ROTC ball and looking for all the world as if he were leaving on the next troop carrier for Bosnia, I said what would probably be considered the wrong thing. Especially because I said it in front of his date.

"Oh, my God! I used to change this boy's diapers."

He was all shoulders and gold braid, all epaulets and brass buttons and not at all the little boy in sleepers to whom I would read stories while his parents slept in.

During recent trips to the hometown where my three sisters live, I have seen with fresh eyes my nephews, who appear to have done nothing but eat and grow since I saw them at Christmas.

Bill is wearing his father's suits and talking his father's brand of politics. Stephen wants to pierce one ear and wear a string tie to church. And John Ford can now tuck his hair behind his ears.

Born in a cluster, these guys are driving and shaving — neither one well nor often — and they are taller than their mothers and better-looking than their dads, and I am stuck thinking of them as little boys. My sisters' babies.

These women and their sons have passed gracefully through a moment that my son and I are fast approaching. That time when we can't make our sons do what we say, and they know it. That point where we both realize that Mom can no longer enforce rules with the force that has always been implied in the tone of her voice.

When one of my nephews — who shall remain nameless — copped an attitude with his mother and used a tone of voice that sent flames of anger up her neck and into her cheeks, she told him in a voice low and steely that she would smack his face if he ever talked like that to her again.

What both knew but did not acknowledge was that she would have to reach up to do that, and he could no doubt stop her hand with the powerful reflexes of his own.

Such face-slapping is rare — perhaps too rare — among a generation of mothers educated to believe that physical force is physical abuse. But since the time when we were advised that if a child refused to dress for nursery school we should simply put him in the car in his pajamas, we have believed that we could impose our will on our children by size alone.

What do you do when your children realize they are bigger than you?

A friend who will soon be the shortest person in a family of three sons says that we must keep talking, even after we realize we can't back it up. Sort of the family version of U.S. currency.

"We have to keep saying it like we mean it," she said.

We must patiently state and restate our standards and our expectations and the limits of our tolerance, because our children are listening, even if they are pretending not to, and they need to know — want to know — where we stand, if only so they can more precisely probe us for weaknesses.

"You can't throw up your hands and quit," she told me. "You can't give up your standards, but you have to articulate them in a nonconfrontational way. They have to be observations instead of directives.

"Such as: 'I really believe it is important to... I really can't approve of that... I'm sure you understand that... Our family has always tried to...'

"Like that."

There is an awkwardness in trying to direct the behavior of someone physically larger. That physical size is what you confront each morning at breakfast, but it is also symbolic of emotional growth, of maturity, and is a warning to us that our children really are separate human beings whom we can no longer control.

Not that we won't continue to try.

Recently, my son, who spends most of his days eating and most of his nights growing, responded to my call for him by saying, "Wha' chew wan', homey?"

Saying it as though I could still make it happen, I told him in a voice low and steely:

"I am not your homey. I am your Mommy. And if you ever call me that again, I will prove it to you by kissing your sweet face in front of any four of your friends."

# Mow, mow, mow your lawn

AS I WRITE this, my husband is cutting the grass.

As you read this, he is probably cutting the grass. Still. Or again.

At this time of year, my husband is usually always cutting the grass.

I am sure it is because the grass is growing, fed by melted snow and spring rains. I am sure it is not personal. I am sure he is not cutting the grass because that is the one place he is certain I will not be. Out there, cutting the grass.

I am sure it is not because he will never hear my voice over the roar of the lawn mower, calling him to dinner.

The grass appears to be most in need of cutting in the moments just before I put dinner on the table. Not just any dinner, but one of the three or four dinners we eat together as a family during any given calendar year. The one dinner I make every quarter or so that does not come from a large plastic bag from Sam's Club.

It is only my husband who cuts the grass. So I have to trust him when he says it needs cutting. If he says it is time to cut the grass, I cannot argue. I cannot push the lawn mower out of the way when I am trying to get an extension cord, so how would I know if it was time to cut the grass?

I could cut the grass if I wanted to learn. I don't. I learned to take the garbage to the curb, and look where that got me. Every Monday and Thursday night, that's me, taking the garbage to the curb. They are right when they say, "A little knowledge is a dangerous thing."

If I learned to cut the grass, that might be me out there, cutting the grass. But at least I wouldn't be doing it just as I was about to put dinner on the table. That would be one advantage to learning to cut the grass. It would never conflict with the special family dinners I plan.

My husband is a friendly, neighborly kind of guy, but don't ask him to lend you his lawn mower. You can ask him to cut your grass, if you like. He would do it cheerfully. But, to be honest, I think he would sooner lend me out to one of the men in the neighborhood than lend his lawn mower. He says that if you lend your lawn mower, it will come back to you with the gas cap missing or a bent blade.

I have wondered if he has any theories about how I would come back.

There is another reason my husband does not lend his lawn mower.

"A lawn mower only has so many cuts in it," he says.

I have to remember to ask him how many cuts that is. I wonder how a man keeps track.

Does he take a jar and put a bean in it every time he cuts his grass during the first summer of his relationship with his lawn mower? Thereafter, does he take a bean out every time he cuts his grass? When the jar is nearly empty, does he know it is time to buy a new lawn mower?

Cutting the grass requires that you know something about spark plugs and gasoline. Specifically, it requires that you know when the spark plugs are dirty and when the lawn mower is out of gas.

Men seem to know these things about their lawn mower without gauges or little stickers on the windshield that tell them the odometer reading necessary for the next oil change. Men can tell these things about their lawn mower without hearing it from some guy with his name stitched on his shirt.

Such intuitive understanding of the parts of a lawn mower is no doubt the result of long hours spent cutting the grass.

If it weren't for me, my husband wouldn't have any grass to cut. It was my idea to sod the yard. It was not my idea to put down the sod on that really rainy day, when each of the sodden rolls of sod weighed about 100 pounds. But I didn't think it would hurt the rooting process.

Anyway, my husband apparently does not like putting down sod as much as he likes cutting the grass that results, because when he was done and he was wet and muddy and irritable, he wondered aloud if the neighbors would notice a 5-foot-9-inch lumpy spot in the yard.

My husband is different from other men because he likes to cut the grass. I am not sure why. For my husband, cutting the grass must be a state of mind instead of a mindless task. I hope that is true. I hope I would marry a man who could be so transported by solitude and not one who just really liked to cut the grass.

Our children are older now, and they require more of my husband's time on weekends. He coaches them in sports that he has not played or in sports in which he has never had success. I have suggested that he teach them to cut the grass. They would benefit from his example of patience in the face of such a numbing task.

Better still, I said, why don't you hire someone to cut the grass? We would have more time to do things as a family. Go out to dinner, perhaps.

He bristled at the suggestion. He was very offended. "How would you feel if I suggested that we pay some stranger to come into your kitchen and whip up a meal?" he asked.

"That's not a bad idea," I replied.

"We'd only need to do it three or four times a year."

# 5 secrets of highly successful husbands

WE KNOW THIS much about husbands: They didn't do it on purpose. They weren't thinking when they did it. They are sorry, and they want to make it up to us.

That, and they don't know what they did.

A husband can tell when his wife is hurt or angry, and that usually means he did something wrong. God knows what it was.

But that doesn't matter anymore, because now he has to make it better. A husband will do anything to make it better, because if she is hurt or angry, he has failed. Failed to make her happy.

Men don't like failing. At anything. Certainly not at being a husband. Men like success, and they want to be successful husbands. But it is their wives who must tell them how.

"Guys love to go bowling because they know where the pins are," says Rob Becker, whose one-man stage show, "Defending the Caveman," does more to explain the origins of men than all the jawbones in all the archaeological dirt piles in all the world.

"There's nothing a guy loves to do more than bowl with his buddies. But take a drape and put it in front of the pins and a guy won't know where the pins are and he won't know if he's knocked any down.

"Do that, and he's not gonna go bowling anymore.

"A woman's gotta tell a guy where the pins are, and she's gotta tell him when he's knocked them down."

So, as our gift to men on Father's Day, we have gathered all the pins, and we will set them up for you.

We talked to relationship experts from Becker to Ann Landers. We talked to psychologists who are men and psychologists who are women. We talked to marriage counselors who have been married for 30 years and some who have been married three times. And we talked to plenty of unhappy wives — and bewildered husbands.

Some themes emerged, some truths surfaced. We have culled their wisdom and arranged it for you in a simple, easy-to-read guide. We call it: "The Five Secrets of Highly Successful Husbands."

Make that "Occasionally Successful." Or "Successful That One

Time." Or "Might Be Successful, But We're Not Saying For Sure."

Because even if you incorporate these secrets into your daily living, you might not be a successful husband for longer than league night at the local lanes. Successful husbanding is not a static experience or a permanent condition because we will keep moving the pins.

The nature of successful husbanding is fluid; it is constantly changing. Because women like changing men.

That's why we marry them.

### The First Secret: Talk

Tell her your dreams and daydreams. Tell her about the demons that keep you up at night or the empty places in your heart.

If you can't do that, talk to her about your job. Surely, you can think of something to say. Choose a topic from "Jeopardy." Current events, famous families, art history. Anything.

"Women want to sit down and discuss," says William Nordling, clinical director of the National Institute of Relationship Enhancement in Bethesda.

She doesn't want a relationship that is all business, a relationship in which conversation focuses on tasks, schedules and logistics.

She wants to know what you are thinking right now. She wants to know how you feel about her. Women are constantly taking the temperature of their relationships, and they do it with words. They want to be part of a man's interior life — such as it is.

"He has to be a good communicator," says Landers, who has been listening to marital troubles and dispensing advice for 40 years.

But if you don't want to talk, say so. Tell her, "Honey, I had a bad day at the office." Or "Honey, I just need to chill out for a little while." Having survived on less than that for so long, she will be satisfied.

"If men are quiet, it is an invitation for women to interrogate," says marriage and family therapist and author Michele Weiner-Davis of Woodstock, Ill. "Women just want to check in."

For women, conversation is the coin of the realm, and a husband can buy his way out of all sorts of trouble if he just talks to his wife. Sit there like a totem pole and she's going to get angry, or stay angry at you for whatever it was you did. Men think talk is a waste of time until they learn how much it pleases their wives.

If you come up short on verbal intimacy, try gossip. If you can't talk about your own relationship, talk about somebody else's.

"Some couples get along better when they are trashing a third party," says John L. Gottman, marriage researcher at the University of Washington in Seattle.

## The Second Secret: Listen

"I can always tell when my husband is not listening to me," wrote Erma Bombeck, the late queen of domestic comedy. "He either lifts up the phone and dials a number, walks out of the room or gets in the car and drives away.

"He's rather typical of most men who ask, 'What kind of a day did you have?' before they go into the bathroom with a newspaper."

One of the major complaints of women in therapy — and women who aren't — is that their husbands don't listen to them.

He might pretend to listen. He might use the mute button on the remote control while she's talking. But when he doesn't respond to her in complete sentences, she knows he is faking it.

He can't help it. He is afraid to listen. Afraid to hear that he is the source of her pain. He thinks it is safer to sit like a fence post while she vents and to pretend that he is hearing her.

"If her husband fails to respond, eventually she will shut down," warns Weiner-Davis, who wrote "Divorce-Busting" for couples at just such a crossroads.

"She will think, 'I'm outta here.' She has already developed her own exit strategy. She stops complaining, and he thinks everything is all right. But really, she has stopped being there."

But responding to her with a solution is as dangerous to your marriage as not responding at all. Your Mr. Fix-It instinct will be your undoing because she doesn't hear a solution. She hears you cutting her off. She hears you belittling her problem. She hears you dismissing her.

This listening thing is much, much harder than you think. Conversation with your wife is a minefield because you must not only hear what she says, but also what she means. You must hear what she is feeling, what she is not saying.

It isn't fair, but women don't always say what they want. To continue Becker's perfect analogy, she doesn't always say which pins you have to knock down, much less where they are.

She wants you to know.

## The Third Secret: Anticipate

Men require specification and negotiation, says Becker, spokesman for half the human race.

"You tell me what you want and I'll tell you what I'll give you and we'll argue about it," he says.

"I used to think women wanted you to guess. 'You give it to me before I ask for it and I'll judge the results.' "

But Becker was wrong, and he knows that now. "Women don't want us to guess. They want us to know. The answer should flow from us naturally. The chemistry is so good, we are doing exactly what they would have done."

Women do not ask for this because they are spoiled or contrary. They are not administering a test of love: "If you loved me, you'd know. If I have to tell you, you must not love me."

It is because women spend their days anticipating the needs of infants and children that they assume any halfway intelligent adult male ought to be able to know how to care for his wife.

Becker says women should lay it all out for a guy. Give him a task, give him a list. Tell him what to do, and you will be surprised at how happy he is to do it because it is making you happy.

But there is a reason why women require this diabolical mind-reading. It is a sign to her that you understand her, that you are attentive to her.

She thinks she is tossing out cues the size of manhole covers, and you don't know what she takes in her coffee. You've lived with her for 15 years and, like the husband in Anne Tyler's "Ladder of Years," you couldn't describe her for a missing person's report.

She can only conclude that she married a complete stone-head.


### The Fourth Secret: Romance

It is how you won her, and it is how you will keep her.

You think there is no statute of limitations with a woman? That any grievance, no matter how ancient, is fresh pain to her?

Wait until you see how long she holds on to the gossamer memories of your courtship. Trust us: She remembers every minute of it.

But if you settle into a partnership with her, into a division of labor, into co-existence, you will wake up one morning to find that your parallel lives don't intersect.

A California study demonstrated that sexual betrayal or fighting were not the most frequent cause of divorce. Most divorcing couples blamed a gradual growing apart and a loss of closeness.

"The absence of conflict doesn't mean romance," says Diane Sollee, founder of the Coalition for Marriage, Family and Couples Education in Washington. "It would be nice. But women want more. They want actual romance."

Romancing a woman is not as simple as sending flowers. Sad to say, a woman sees this not as an offering of love, but as the no-brain response of a man vaguely aware that he is in some kind of trouble.

Any idiot can send flowers. You'd score more points if you bought her a pair of sexy sandals because you know her shoe size. Or if you buy her a CD because you remember what music she sings along with in the car. Or if you know the names of her girlfriends and can keep them straight.

In short, you must do something that tells her she is not a generic woman, but a woman about whom you know intimate things.

And romance is more than telling her she looks nice. You must let her know that you desire her, that the parts of her body she wants to conceal under clothing are not just acceptable, but intoxicating.

But love-making is not an excuse not to talk.

"Love talk," says Weiner-Davis. "Women need love talk."

Every therapist tells some version of the story about the man who loved his wife so much, he almost told her. But "I love you," only works on little candy hearts. A woman wants to know how, why. She wants supporting details, examples, elaborations.

Do this, and wait to see how she says, "I love you, too." We promise, she won't use words.


### The Fifth Secret: Be Flexible

In the past, marriage was a vehicle for fulfilling a role, says Bernard Guerney Jr., a pioneer in marriage therapy. Woman was nurturer and hearth-keeper; man was breadwinner.

"If you did your job, it was a good marriage," says Guerney.

But the movement of women and mothers into the work force and the women's liberation movement have caused the earth to shift under marriage.

"Now roles aren't culturally clear, and they are subject to conflict," says Guerney, founder of the National Institute of Relationship Enhancement in Bethesda.

"Everything is up for grabs."

But the war between the sexes is not about chores; it just seems that way.

Our expectations of each other are tangled up in our dreams and aspirations, in our family history, in Bible stories and in gender politics. All these things supercharge the workings of a household.

The roles of husband and wife have merged and blended in lots of very good ways — ask any woman whose husband pays more attention to their children than her father paid to her. We are more like interchangeable "co-spouses."

The result is, the messages you receive from your wife are going to continue to be very confused. We want you to nurture the children and we want you to initiate sex. We want you to carve the turkey, cut the grass and change the flat tire, but don't expect us to have dinner on the table every night at 5.

We want you to be our soul mate, but we wouldn't have married you if we didn't want a man around the house.

"I don't think women want men to lose their masculine roles, but they don't see that as incompatible with sharing their emotional lives," says Nordling.

Get it? Do both, be everything.

That's the secret.

Happy Father's Day.

# We'll talk . . . later

TWO WEEKS AGO, in the Father's Day edition of this newspaper, I offered what I thought was gentle insight about what women want from the fathers of their children.

After probing the experiences of marriage counselors, advice columnists, stand-up comics and the women around me, I concluded that fathers who are also husbands should strive to communicate better, to continue to romance the women they once courted so lovingly and to remain flexible as men's and women's roles continued to change.

Because Father's Day is just about the only day a man can be sure he will not be in trouble with his wife — women love rituals and traditions and preserve them jealously — I thought I was doing a service by offering men a means to maintain peace the other 364.

Wrong.

The overwhelming response was that the article was poorly timed, insensitive and inappropriate for the day when we celebrate the role of the man in family life.

"Why did you pick Father's Day?" male readers asked.

This response is a variation of "Do we have to talk about this now?" It is the first of a series of responses that continue with "What does it take to make you happy?" and "What are you trying to say? That you want a divorce?" It is a singular mix of avoidance followed by overreaction that men do so well.

I was trying to be nice, but it is clear that my suggestions were seen as attacks. Why would I pick Father's Day to lay another lecture, like a lash, across the backs of men?

OK. When would be a good time?

When should we get back to you? Can you pencil us in? Are you free for lunch on the 19th? Can we get our people to call your people and set something up? Let us know when you have a minute to talk. Get your datebook and give us a call back.

The question, "Why Father's Day?" presupposes that there is another day that would have been better. What would that day be? Labor Day?

Good Friday? Doris Day?

My guess is, no day is the best day.

When I tell my husband I need to talk to him, he folds his arms across his chest, looks away sharply and sternly and says, "What topic?" The rough translation of this body language is barbed wire and guns.

It is clear men do not believe conversation with women can be benign or without consequences. They want to be warned that conversation is on the horizon so they can brace for it. All women have seen this. Tell him you'd like to go out to dinner or go for a walk and just talk and he will want to know what's wrong.

There is no good time to talk to a man about matters of the heart.

Not before he's had his first cup of coffee and not when he is just about to fall asleep for the night. Not when he is on his way out the door and certainly not the minute he walks in.

Not before he has had sex, and not after he's had sex.

Even when he says in frustration, "Just tell me what you want," you know he doesn't want you actually to tell him.

Don't tell him on the phone. And not in front of the kids. Not where the neighbors might hear. Not while he is eating, not while he is trying to drive and not while the game is on.

Not when he is reading the paper. Not when he's shaving. Not while the two of you are getting dressed to go out and certainly not on the way to the party.

No time is the right time to talk to a man.

I should have known that meant Father's Day, too.

# Chapter 4

# Kids:
*The Instruction Book*

# Queen Mother

"I AM THE Queen," she said. "Everything you need to know starts with that fact."

Standing over her kitchen sink, her anger and agitation churning the soapy water, she was washing dishes and recounting to me the moment when her relationship with her children had changed.

Not right away, perhaps. It occurred to me that they might have recognized the scene she was describing as the periodic price of doing business with Mom and kept their heads down until it was over.

But for this woman, it was life-changing. She was Copernicus, telling the world that the sun did not revolve around it, but it around the sun.

"I am not a doormat or a domestic servant. I am not a helpmate or a handmaiden. I am not your own personal cheerleading section," she had told them.

"I am the queen of your world. I am She Who Must Be Obeyed.

"I am the straw that stirs the drink. I am da man. I am the be-all and end-all for all of you."

That is what she told them the morning she found all those clean clothes in the hamper, the results of sartorial indecision someone was too lazy to return to the dresser.

The morning she found the cap missing from the root beer and the carton of melted ice cream in the cupboard where she keeps the drinking glasses.

The morning she found all those plastic sleeves from freeze pops littering the carpet in front of the television like freshly cut hay.

The morning she realized that her family might only be able to describe her in the negative, by listing all the things that were not done when she was gone.

"I am the reason there is always more toilet paper under the bathroom sink," she told them. "I am the reason there is always more ketchup in the pantry.

"I am the reason none of you has measles, mumps or rubella," she said. "I make it happen around here. I grease the skids in your happy little lives. I feed you, I clothe you, I comfort you. I sign you up and then

I drive you there, and I am not waiting any longer for you to notice. "You guys will worship the ground I walk on, and it will start now." She demanded that they do what she could not get done and express their gratitude for what she did. She no longer asked for "help," because that implied the job was hers, done by them only as a favor or an act of generosity.

So she assigned tasks, and if they whined, or did them too poorly or too slowly, she assigned more tasks. They were indentured servants for weeks before they realized that she wasn't kidding.

They were teen-agers, for goodness' sake, and if they could not manage the clothing in their lives, she would pack it away until they could, leaving them with two choices: the clean outfit or the dirty one.

These were not chores, they were responsibilities. And there were no cash bonuses, no praise, no good-job kisses for their completion.

For years, she had hustled to meet their expectations of her. Now, they would live up to her expectations of them, or no one would ever go to the movies or horseback riding again.

Her face turned the color of her hands in the hot water as she remembered the scene from months ago. It had been no outburst, but an epiphany, the moment when she realized that she was a parent, not a character from "Remains of the Day."

She would no longer spend every day postponing her existence until her children left for college or volunteered to load the dishwasher.

During a weekend visit, I saw that the queen's new law had been written on the hearts of her people. Tasks were done without complaint, and the family machine worked relatively smoothly.

I also saw a mother who was no longer a martyr but a manager — delegating, not doing it all.

My own children, the little prince and princess to whom I had played the part of chambermaid for so long, did not see these things, and they flinched with surprise when, upon returning home, I declared:

"I am the queen. Everything you need to know starts with that fact."

# From another vantage point, the kids are all right

"ALL YOU HAVE to do is drink soda for two hours and smile when your aunts start squealing about how much you've grown," I said.

"That, and wear a shirt with a collar."

These were my son's marching orders for the recent holidays. A fairly painless prescription for passing the time among relatives he sees once a year.

My daughter's instructions were pretty much the same.

"All you have to do is drink soda for two hours and smile when your aunts tell you how pretty you've become," I said.

"That, and wear your sweat shirt right side out."

These things they did well as my husband and I dragged their teen-aged selves from reunion to reunion. They still looked bored to my practiced eye, but I don't think anyone else noticed.

And, I must say, I have not liked my children so much since the same time last year.

There is nothing like seeing your kids through someone else's eyes to change your view of them.

Suddenly, he did look much taller and she, much prettier. Both were shyly polite and smiled disarmingly at their uncles and cousins. And "used all our manners," as my daughter once said upon entering a white-linen restaurant.

Away from my crowded kitchen at dinner time, away from their friends, away from school and just beyond my reach, my children were bathed in a new light and I saw them differently.

I saw them as other people see them.

And they were not irritating, bickering, rude, clueless and uncooperative.

They were very nice kids, deserving of all the standard compliments lavished upon them by the relatives who do not have to finish a science project with them the night before it is due.

There is nothing like a fresh perspective on teen-agers you might have been close to strangling during the previous week.

I ran into a fellow mother at parent-teacher conferences recently, and was surprised to see her there because her middle-school son is known to be an excellent student and never a discipline problem.

I asked if there was a problem, and she said, exhaling the words in a confessional rush, "I just wanted to hear somebody say something nice about him."

Of course. I should have guessed. That's why I was there, too. I wanted to hear something good about my kids because, like my friend, I couldn't think of anything at the moment.

It is no wonder that the parents in the thick of raising teen-agers can't see the good in them; the dust of battle never settles long enough. Even the mildest kids thrive on argument. Parents are constantly amazed at the topics up for debate:

Proper personal hygiene and the amount of time and hot water it takes to achieve it.

The role of the parent in wish-fulfillment.

The quality of food served in the home, and whether the folks at Sam's Club or the boys behind the counter at Domino's might do a better job.

Clothing — whether it fits correctly, is in style or requires immediate washing. And whether it is more efficiently stored on the floor of one's room.

The value of education, and whether the parent shows any sign of having had any.

The finite funds that flow into the house, how they should be allocated, and whether anything resembling chores should be required in exchange.

Your personal child-rearing style, your home's similarity to a gulag, and whether the children could get a better deal in foster care.

If you have teen-agers, you wake up to an argument and you fall asleep with the last argument ringing in your tired ears. It is either that, or your personal teen-ager is setting a new standard for "sullen," one that will stand for all time.

It is hard to find something nice to say about them when you are having trouble thinking of a reason to go on living.

My advice?

Put yourself across a crowded room from them. Preferably, one filled with adults who, by birth or marriage, are predisposed to like them for your sake. And watch them.

From this perspective, your children will look taller or more handsome. Prettier than ever and more mature. Sweet and polite.

"Delightful kids. Just delightful." You will hear it said, and you will have to agree.

"I hugged your Joseph and he hugged me back. First time ever," my sister wrote in a holiday postscript.

"I think he is going to be just fine."

And from where she stood, I, too, could see that he would be just fine.

# A leap of faith

I DON'T THINK I'm Christian. It was one of those conversational hand grenades that middle-schoolers so often toss at their parents.

In the midst of their grousing and grouching, about the time you are turning a deaf ear to their attempts to provoke you, middle-schoolers will say something that tells you their stomachs are not the only part of them that is churning these days.

"Joe," I said, "religion is not like a college major. You don't get to switch just because you are bored or failing organic chemistry.

"Besides, we are in the fourth quarter of Catholicism here. Two more years, and you will be confirmed. If you decide to be Jewish or Buddhist, you're going to have to start all over again."

"I just don't know if I believe any of it," he said. "The Bible stories seem like they are just stories to me. Like somebody made them up for people too dumb to understand stuff like evolution. How can you tell if there is a God?"

That a crisis of faith should strike Joe was no surprise, considering his most recent dealings with God.

A grandfather, a grandmother, the father of a boy his own age — blameless, benevolent figures in his life — had died. The father of his best friend was battling cancer, and so was a sweet, baby girl "cousin."

Where was God in all of this? Joe must have felt that there was nobody on the other end of the phone.

Even before Joe's faith, such as it is, was tested by tragedy, he was bored by religion. As soon as they stopped making crafts and serving snacks in Sunday school, as soon as they tried to teach instead of entertain, Joe and his friends began their rebellion.

Every Sunday morning in more households than mine, there are arguments unfit for those preparing for worship, and families go to meet God in a fury. Adolescents storm off to class and parents kneel in church, flushed, sweating, their minds fogged with a mix of anger and regret.

This has probably been true since Abraham's time. I can imagine Isaac dawdling and complaining all the way to the top of the mountain. Nothing is more boring to adolescents than the preaching of adults.

Joe has tried everything to pass the time in Sunday school — drawing elaborate doodles on his book or the palm of his hand, pulling out hidden soldiers or airplanes from his pockets.

I was suspicious of his cheerful cooperation last Sunday and then found that had wired himself for sound.

Joe had tucked a radio in his jeans and run a tiny earpiece up the sleeve of his shirt and out his cuff. He sat with his cheek resting on the palm of his hand, listening to sports talk shows. His gleeful confession after church made me laugh in spite of myself.

Joe is not the only bored teen-ager in church, and I am not the only mother praying for patience. The conveyance of faith to the next generation is not going smoothly in any household I know.

A friend who is the mother of four bailed out of organized religion after the first bat mitzvah nearly killed her. She could not imagine doing it three more times. Now she spends Sunday mornings teaching her children to clean house. She feels that she is conveying a life skill — and she has something to show for it. As distasteful as this is for the kids, it goes more smoothly than getting out the door for Hebrew school ever did.

Another woman friend shares Joe's uncertainty about the nature of God and isn't sure exactly what it is she is supposed to tell her children. She goes to church, and she gets the kids there as often as she is up for the battle. On her judgment day, she plans to tell St. Peter: "Hey, I'm sorry if I didn't get it, but I showed up. I was there."

But many more of my friends can think of nothing more unholy than to be trapped on narrow, hard benches with bored children in dress clothes.

Sunday mornings in those homes are languid and peaceful, scented with fresh coffee and the envy of the rest of us. A day of newspapers, soft music and a modest household chore or two seems heavenly to dual-career, rec-league sports parents who, unlike God, do not give themselves a day of rest.

"Joe," I said, turning my mind to the task his declaration presented me, "Whatever you think of the story of Noah's Ark or the story of Easter, you have to admit Jesus didn't have any bad ideas.

"Hang in there until you've learned what he had to teach about how people should live with each other. Then you will be confirmed, we will have a big party, you will make your grandmother cry happy tears and you will get lots of presents."

What I did not tell Joe was that confirmation will not resolve the debate going on inside his head over whether he is a Christian, whether the Bible stories are more than stories.

It is merely a bon voyage party for his awakening soul, the send-off for a journey that will last his whole life.

# Hard days, nights

IN BILL WATTERSON'S comic strip "Calvin & Hobbes," Calvin, the little boy who is every mother's worst nightmare, tells his stuffed buddy Hobbes that he knows his purpose on Earth.

That purpose, Calvin says, is to make everybody do what he wants.

"That about sums it up," a friend said to me. "That is a difficult child."

She is the mother of a "difficult child" or a "willful child" or a "challenging child" depending on the parenting book currently open on her night table. She has read them all, and none, she said, captured her child as crisply as that cartoon.

This 10-year-old dictates everything from the family grocery list to the family vacation. Why? "Peace at all costs," said my battle-weary friend.

He's starving when she is on the phone, not hungry when dinner is on the table. He will not give up his sweat pants in the spring or his shorts when the first frost arrives. "I don't like the way these things feel," he tells her, writhing as if his skin were on fire.

He doesn't want to do his homework now. He doesn't want to take a bath now. If it is Sunday, he doesn't want to go to church. "He's on an eight-hour delay," his father says.

If it is time for soccer, he doesn't want to practice. "What's the point?" he says. "We're going to lose." He's Mr. Negative.

Each morning he asks: "What is our plan for today?" And if it changes, he explodes in anger.

He badgers her constantly, renegotiating his punishments, the house rules, even dinner reservations.

"He is relentless. He never gives in. He never backs down," she says.

She is defeated, depressed, and her confidence in her parenting skills is shot. Her discipline is all up and down the scale. She is dizzy from her flights to anger and remorse and back again.

His father is baffled, she told me. He sees none of his easygoing self in the child. He is angry that she cannot keep the family peace. Every night, he comes home to the remains of a new battle — a fresh set of tears to wipe. Two warring parties fuming at opposite ends of his house. His sister is practicing to be the perfect child. She sees what happens when you are not.

He is not a bad seed. He is wonderful in school, a loyal friend and a delight around other parents. So insightful that his mother thinks he can see into the hearts of others. But their family life has always been a tangle of emotions, and now he is getting a very smart mouth.

"I have read all the books and tried all the management techniques — the charts, the stickers," she says. "I have canceled everything in his life but Christmas. I have told him he is grounded until his senior prom. He never backs down, and nothing ever changes.

"I know I need to be 'consistent.' That's what all the books say. I need to follow through. But I can't take the battles. Then I start thinking about what he will be like when he has a set of car keys, and I panic and think I can never give in to him again."

She talks to every friend she has, hoping one will say something that will open a door to the solution: a new attitude she can take with him that will calm the storms between them. Finally, one does.

"She told me I have to look at consistency and control in a new way."

The rules don't change — that is the consistency, her friend told her. You may fight about homework and back talk tonight, but tomorrow the same rules will be in place. You have to believe that he is internalizing these rules, even if all he does is resist them and try to renegotiate them.

Be consistent about fewer things, she said. Pick a few battles you have to win, walk away from the rest.

And you have to think of him the way you thought of him when he was 2, her friend told her. You can't control him any more now than you could then, but you did not blame him then and you are blaming him now.

It is his temperament. It is the way he came. It is the way he is wired. He is not doing these things to punish you or to drive you crazy. And, more important, he is not doing them because of your lousy parenting. He is the way he is.

"And she taught me a new way to look at consistency. That I have to make it clear to him that every tomorrow will be a new day, a new chance for success, a starting over. That the anger of the day before disappears in the night.

"She told me that I have to love him again every morning.

"I can do that," she says. "I can do that."

# Virtuosity

WHEN I REALIZED that I needed to teach my children values, in addition to how to cut their meat and how to ride a two-wheeler, I did what over-involved mothers such as me usually do.

I bought a book.

I bought "The Book of Virtues: A Treasury of Great Moral Stories," a compendium of 370 fables, poems, essays and stories collected by former Secretary of Education and drug czar William J. Bennett and divided into chapters with titles such as "Self-discipline," "Compassion," "Work" and "Courage."

Here, then, was the perfect way to convey a value system to my children. I would simply read to them at night — by the 800-page thickness of the book, it would be many nights — and when I was done, I would have instilled in them the values that Dr. Bennett, at least, thought they should have.

I began by reading the story of the little Dutch boy and the dike, under the chapter heading "Perseverance," because we were having trouble in our house sticking to tasks.

But after I read the dramatic account of the little boy who kept his finger in a hole in the dike all night long and saved his village, my son screwed up his face and said:

"That's dumb. Why did they build a dike out of dirt that is going to crack like that. Why didn't they call in the Army Corps of Engineers to build a real dike?"

Why do it yourself, he seemed to have concluded, when you can get a government agency to do it for you?

Teaching values, I thought, is slippery business. The word itself sounds kind of square. Like a preacher talking. But thanks to President Clinton and his politics of meaning, it is now safe for some of us to come out from under the cabbage leaves and use the word "values" without being dismissed as a devotee of the religious right.

For years, we have said nothing at all — a new kind of Silent Majority — fearing that whatever we said would be a judgment of others the likes of which we would never tolerate if leveled against us.

How could we disapprove of out-of-wedlock births without seeming to condemn the valiant single mom to whom her successful children point as their inspiration?

How could we condemn the faithless father without acknowledging that government rewards the mother and his child with more benefits if he splits?

How can we condemn illegitimacy without stigmatizing the blameless child?

And so we have treated whatever values we held like some private thing that never sees the light of day. Something you don't talk about in mixed company.

But we have children now, and they are our stake in the world, and we have to dust off our values and start applying them to issues that will affect their lives.

One of those issues is sex.

We felt like we discovered it. We certainly revolutionized it. Now that revolution is over. It ended when we realized that some day our baby daughters would date. It ended when we realized they could get pregnant on one of those dates.

The pendulum has swung back, and we are riding it. The country has concluded that teen-age pregnancy is the inexorable result of teen-age sex, and teen-age mothers are not good mothers. We have also concluded that children are better off with two parents. The logic of this syllogism is inescapable: Don't have sex until you are a grown-up, and don't have children until you are married. And don't get divorced.

Wow. We will feel like Alice-through-the-looking-glass preaching this line to our children.

And it will not work if it is our only message, if abstinence is the only thing we preach. That's not so much a virtue as it is the result of virtues. Virtues such as courage and responsibility.

We can all agree on the worth of Dr. Bennett's chapter headings, but teaching faith, loyalty, work, compassion — that is something else altogether. How do you know when your children have learned them? Must you wait 20 years and see what they are like as adults?

President Clinton is not just using the lectern like a pulpit and preaching to Americans about these values; he and his advisers are fashioning what they hope will be a comprehensive "family policy," and its principles will show up in the health care, welfare and crime legislation he will send to Congress this year.

Whew. It will get mighty crowded in my son's bed at night — me and a raft of government advisers trying to teach him his values. The idea of politicians — even Bill Clinton, a politician with whom I often agree — issuing family values as government policy makes the hair on the back of my neck stand up.

The real lesson I learned when I read the story of the little Dutch boy and the dike to Joseph is this: There is no book of virtues. There is no one place where they are all kept, no place where they are all arranged in neat categories.

And there are no flashcards for virtues, I learned. No after-school program for virtues. No sleep-over summer camp for virtues. I know. I checked. And my guess is, you will never find them in a government white paper, either.

If there is a simple way to instill in children the qualities that will keep them happy and help them contribute to the world while doing no harm to others, I have not found it.

# Take this job and show it

IN VIRGINIA LAST week, a man was arrested for impersonating a deputy U.S. marshal during talks he gave at his children's school.

He showed up at Hylton High School in Dale City, Va., with a 9mm handgun and a bulletproof vest, a cap and a jacket with "U.S. MARSHAL" patches on them, and he wowed his children's classmates.

Whether he ever was a U.S. deputy marshal is in doubt. But school officials accused him of being a fraud, and now this father faces a possible sentence of five years in prison for carrying a gun on school property.

Poor guy. I know just how he feels.

It is pretty tough when your kids are unimpressed — no, embarrassed — by what you do to earn money to pay for all their stuff.

Remember the scene in the movie "City Slickers"? Billy Crystal, who buys commercials for a radio station ("I sell air time. I sell air. What is that?" he asks), visits his son's school for Career Day. Nine-year-old Danny introduces his father as a submarine commander.

During my previous incarnation as a sportswriter, my kids were proud of me on Career Day. My son thought it was cool that his mom covered sports, and all the kids loved my stuff. You know, my press passes, NFL press guides, a portable phone, a portable computer, a tape recorder. I taught them how to score a baseball game and told them I discovered David Robinson, who once played basketball for the Naval Academy but is now just the hottest thing in the NBA. I was sensational.

Now that I am a columnist, I am not even going to Career Day. What would I say to impress them? "Ummm. They give me this whole, you know, uhhh, column of space in the paper, and I, uhh, you know, write stuff I think about. Any questions?"

"National humiliation," is how my 10-year-old son, who often appears in this space, describes my job.

My friend Reid Cherner, who edits sports for *USA Today*, and I'm sure does a darn fine job, shares my feelings. He knows that he is a professional liability to his kids. He found that out when he went to their preschool to give a talk titled, "Your friend, the First Amendment."

He followed a guy with a hawk.

When he complained to the teacher about the poor scheduling, she told him: "Oh, don't worry. The children are very excited today. As soon as you're done, we are going to hear from a policeman."

There's that gun thing again.

"My daughter, Hannah, asked me what I was doing there," Reid says. "I told her I came to talk to her class about my job. She's been to my office 50 times, but she says to me, 'Oh, you're going to talk to us about being a dentist?' "

The first thing Reid did after his talk was complain to the school administration that live animals should not be allowed in the school. The second thing he did was make an appointment for Hannah with a dentist.

Reid and I are miserable showmen for our profession, but somebody should give these schoolkids a look at the world of newspapers. So I sent my husband, Gary, fresh from the Olympics, to talk to the kids' physical education classes about what he had seen and done in Norway. When I asked how it went, he said: "Oh. Fine." That was all.

Then the obligatory thank-you notes started to arrive from the children. They all said pretty much the same thing: "Dear Mr. Mihoces: Thank you for teaching us about the Olympics. We liked it when you danced. We hope you come back soon with your dancing."

"Dancing?" I asked. "You danced?"

He mumbled in reply.

"Excuse me, but you didn't even dance at our wedding and you are doing some kind of Olympic dance for schoolkids?" I said, my voice rising now. "What dance?"

Turns out it was a dance Norwegians did to keep warm while watching Olympic events in the bitter cold. My children's father set the school abuzz with this Norwegian warm-up dancing. The P.E. teacher stopped me at the grocery store to tell me how she had entertained dinner guests with the story of his dancing. Great.

My son wasn't even embarrassed. Well, not too embarrassed. "Dear Dad," his thank-you note began. "Thank you for talking to us. My favorite part was, yes, the dance. I think you made some people learn a little about Norway. Try to keep it more to learning, not dancing."

I'll never be able to top my husband's Career Day act, I know. Not unless columnists start carrying guns.

# Fear itself

BRING BACK FEAR!

Thanks to William Bennett and cover stories on major news magazines, we have already brought back shame.

The shame of having a child out of wedlock, the shame of not supporting him. The shame of living on welfare, the shame of driving drunk, the shame of cheating on your spouse or your taxes or your boss.

The old-fashioned mortification that comes with sin, itself an old-fashioned notion in revival, is back in vogue.

Now that shame is no longer considered a disabling emotion destructive to self-esteem, parents can confidently shame their kids as they go about the business of making them responsible members of society.

Emboldened by the successful return of shame, I volunteer to lead the campaign to restore fear among children.

I've already called Bill Bennett to let him know he can count on me to do this, to rescue fear from its place of neglect and disrepute, to return fear to the American family, to set a place for fear at the American dinner table.

Not the monster-under-the-bed, bogyman variety of fear.

Your kids will keep you up all night with those kinds of fears.

I'm talking about fear of authority. Fear of consequences. The kind of fear that will keep you up all night if your children don't have it.

The kind of unexamined, nonspecific fear we grew up with. The fear behind the refrain of our youth: "My mother will kill me if I..."

We never knew how our mothers would kill us or how these women would explain our sudden disappearance to family and friends. And our mothers never said, "I will kill you if you..." There was no list of offenses. But we knew instinctively when we were approaching an act to which was ascribed the death penalty.

I want that for my children.

I want them to live in fear of what I will do if I catch them doing whatever it is they are thinking about doing.

I'm not going to say what those misdeeds might be because I never want to be on record as enumerating them. I might leave one out, and my children might take that as implicit permission, as in: "You never said we couldn't." That kind of thing.

And I want my children to be afraid of more adults than just me.

I can't be everywhere, after all, and my children must believe that all grown-ups are working off the same list of crimes and misdemeanors and any one of them can be counted on to report to me or exact punishment in my stead.

Something along the lines of, "Paul's mother will kill us if we..."

I want my children to be afraid of what their father will do when he gets home. (This will take some work, as it is not now the case. My children consider their father's arrival a death-row phone call from the governor.)

I want my children to be afraid of what the teacher will do when she stops writing on the board, turns around and sees them. Of what she will do if she walks into the bathroom at just the wrong moment. But most of all, I want them to live in stomach-flipping fear of what will happen if they don't do their homework.

And I want the thought of being sent to the principal's office to make them cold and pale with fear.

I want my children to be afraid of the crossing guard and what will happen if they jaywalk on the way to school, of the convenience store cashier and what will happen if they shoplift, of the firemen and what will happen if they play with BIC lighters in the woods.

I want my children to fear the lifeguard and what will happen if they run on the deck or dunk someone at the pool. I want them to fear the coach and what will happen if they pout while he tells them to play left field or back on defense.

I want them to fear the driver of every car when they are riding their bikes.

I want them to be afraid of what will happen if they don't brush their teeth.

I want them to fear every mother on the planet and what will happen if they make that woman's child cry. I want them to fear every father of every girl they ever date.

And at all other times of decision and conscience, I want them to worry about what God would think if he knew what they were doing. Because God will know, even if they fool me.

# Parents' split decision always loss for kids

MY HUSBAND AND I renewed our wedding vows not long ago with a small church service that included the children of our union.

Jessie and I bought special dresses and carried tiny bouquets. Joe got a new outfit and carried the rings as my husband and I pledged our love.

There was a reception, complete with presents, champagne and a big cake. My husband and I went on a second honeymoon and returned with presents.

None of this made any impression on the kids, because they continue to ask if their father and I are going to get divorced.

Without waiting for an answer, they declare in unison that they will elect to live with their father after the split because he rents better movies and lets them roast marshmallows in the fireplace.

I have gotten over the fact that I am viewed as the no-fun, let-me-see-your-homework parent. But I am troubled that the children of a couple that rarely fights (because the dad refuses to be provoked) are worried that they are going to be sleeping in a different house every other week-end and during holidays.

No, I tell them again and again, we are not getting a divorce.

It has been a common misconception that kids bounce back quickly from the trauma of divorce and that they actually flourish after being released from a contentious marriage. But what has come to be considered essential to an adult's happiness — the freedom to change life partners — has been shown to be, in study after study, detrimental to the child.

Children of divorce are usually thrown immediately into a lesser standard of living, if not into poverty. They are neglected emotionally by their overwrought parents. They have difficulty at school because they are distracted and upset. These children feel responsible for the disintegration of their family because it is better than feeling helpless and abandoned.

Even if divorce is a welcome end to fighting, even if the children understand, even if the parents divorce gently, the kids forever regret not having had an intact family. Long into their own adulthood, children of divorce are found to be depressed, troubled, drifting and under-achieving. They have difficulty making emotional commitments, forming a marriage, holding a job.

In short, children are more likely to recover from your death than your divorce. At least insurance and Social Security can provide some economic stability. And for the child, there is no burden of guilt or unrequited hope for reunion. There is no anger toward the departed parent.

What all this means is that you can't walk away from your marriage if you have any hope of your kids' turning out OK.

You don't get to leave when you are bored or restless or when you fall in love with someone else. Or when your father dies or you lose your job or you turn 50 and your future seems suddenly short and joyless. And you don't even get to leave if your spouse cheats on you — more than once.

What you do is get help, counseling, mediation. Give your kids an intact home and the tremendous, quantifiable bonus that means for them. Give them a lesson in how to solve a problem, how to try to fix something, how not to walk away.

Men and women must realize "that constantly fluctuating perceptions of a mate are essentially illusions . . . and that these illusions can do harm," as Robert Wright writes on infidelity in a recent issue of *Time*. Chasing these illusions is a luxury you do not have when you have children. The kids will be lost while you are trying to find yourself.

This is easy for me to say. I'm married to a great guy who does all the science fair projects, only spends money on gasoline and coffee and whose only sin is that he doesn't put the vacuum cleaner away after he runs it. He doesn't have a bowling night, let alone another woman.

And I could never tell a woman to stay with a man who is beating her or the children or who is sexually abusing them. Those women and children are in danger.

But children of broken marriages are in danger, too. More danger than they face in a home with tension or grudges or a disaffected parent.

It is never better for those kids if the parents divorce. It is only different.

# A poor start

WHEN A TEEN-AGE girl decides to have a baby, it is not just her problem or her mother's problem or a welfare problem.

Very soon, it will be a teacher's problem.

Nowhere is the impact of this young girl's decision more visible, more compelling than in schools. When young girls have babies, they interrupt or abbreviate their own educations. And so the education of their babies is off to the worst possible start.

"School is like a story that most parents start telling their children when they are very young," a teacher says. "They tell what school is going to be like for them, and so the children understand what will happen when they come to us. For most of the children I see, that story never gets told."

She has taught for 17 years in Maryland and West Virginia, in very poor neighborhood schools and in very wealthy ones. Today, she teaches in Maryland. Most of her children are poor, and most have just a mother or a grandmother to go home to. Do not use my name, she asks, protecting the privacy of the children to whom she is achingly devoted.

As a kindergarten teacher, she sees these children fresh, before the world and the educational system have a chance to defeat them.

But she also sees the hundreds of little missing pieces in their lives, and so her job changes daily, fractured through a prism of deprivation.

It is hard to read a story about lima beans, she says, if no one knows what a lima bean is. It is hard to play a game of rhyming words when no one has heard Mother Goose rhymes.

Her abbreviated kindergarten day with these children is a window into their life away from school. The morning children are exhausted, she says, because the early bedtimes are lost when Mom has worked all day and has to do her shopping at night, or when Mom doesn't mind if you are up late watching TV. The afternoon children, fresh from some makeshift day care where marathon videos and unstructured chaos are the norm, are wired.

"They love school and they love me and they want to do anything I ask them," she says. "But when they arrive at school like this, they cannot attend to anything."

Food, too, is a reason they are so frantic, she says. Children are not hungry. School breakfasts and school lunches have solved that.

But, the teacher says, the children are fueled by junk food, their miniature systems flooded by sugar, salt, caffeine and a hundred colorings and preservatives. "We talk about food a lot, and all I ever hear is pizza, hot dogs, chicken nuggets and soda." No lima beans.

The children can't sit still. They don't know how to be part of a group. They can't follow simple directions. They don't recognize that the teacher is in charge or how they are supposed to respond to her. The teacher ticks off the list on her fingers.

"We are not teaching them, we are managing them."

The children come to school worried, too, she says. How incongruous to see grown-up strain in little faces.

"They know what is going on at home. They know Mom needed to pay a bill but spent the money on clothes instead, and they are worried about what will happen. They know that Mom is dating and there is another new man in her life."

Her hands wring absently in her lap as she talks.

"We grew up in an era where whatever Mom did and said was right. They tell me these things, and so I try to explain that sometimes grownups make bad choices, that it is not the child's fault, that they are not responsible for what Mom is doing. They need to hear that."

The miniature homework assignments she gives rarely get done. The books the children check out of the library don't leave their backpacks.

"I tell them that their homework tonight is to find somebody to read that book to them," she says.

There is little, if any, communication between teacher and Mom.

"Maybe she's just too stressed out or she's too embarrassed to get help for the child. Maybe she had a bad experience with school and doesn't want to deal with me," the teacher says.

Cleanliness is a problem, and so this teacher spends a lot of time washing hands and faces and talking about why. "It is hard for them if their clothes aren't clean or their hair isn't combed. They look different and it sets them apart and they know it. Even if they are little, they know it."

And talking. She does so much talking.

"It is almost like counseling, this whole group talking that we do every day. We talk about classroom routines and how you treat your neighbor. We talk about feelings and how you handle them. We do a lot of role-playing and cooperative games.

"I do this because they aren't able to go home to a parent and pour out their day and talk about what happened. And if you can't do that, it comes out in anger."

The talking she does fills another gap, too. Language. When scolding and back talk dominate the conversation at home, a child cannot learn the meaning of words, cannot explain herself or organize her thoughts.

"Or answer a simple question," the teacher says, her voice arching in exasperation. "I know she knows the answer, but she cannot find the words. And if a 5-year-old has the language level of a 2-year-old, you can't expect her to read."

School is a story you tell your children, this kindergarten teacher says. How can any story that begins this way have a happy ending?

Young women are having babies before their own growing up is complete. And they are doing it without a husband, without a partner — a statistical guarantee that mother and child will live in poverty.

# Lessons in black and white

ANNAPOLIS IS LIKE urban centers all over the country. Middle-class families who love the amenities of the city live cheek by jowl with families too poor to escape the mean parts of city life.

At our neighborhood school, children whose parents are both doctors or lawyers learn beside children whose dads are gone. Kids who take sailing lessons play with kids who don't have a family car.

My children go to that school instead of the many private schools that seem to spring up around upper-income city dwellers. I am often asked why. It is a question I often ask myself.

Neither my husband nor I is a product of private schools, so I guess there is an inherent belief that public schools can turn out productive adults. And public schools have vast resources. Even small class size is not a lure to private schools. Because so many Annapolis children are needy, federal funds keep student-teacher ratios at about 20-to-1 in Annapolis elementary schools.

An important part of our decision is financial. It would cost from $8,000 to $16,000 a year to send our two children to private schools. Even if we could manage to pay that kind of tuition, I am unconvinced that my children's education would be $16,000 better. They have had remarkable teachers and successful school years.

And my aging hippie social agenda played a part in our decision, too. Public school is the real world, and I never wanted to convey to my children the message that they were not part of that world, that they had no responsibility to it.

But I have been naive. The lessons of equality and equal opportunity, the lessons I wanted for them, are not the ones my children are learning at school.

Instead they have learned what poor means, that it is not some obscure condition that will prompt another child to eat your vegetables. They have learned that winter jackets, birthday parties, even school supplies and breakfast at home are luxuries for some children.

They have also learned that some kids never do homework, that some kids behave atrociously in class. They have learned not to take things they care about to school because they might disappear.

My daughter learned that not all families have a car or a telephone and thus her good friend could neither get to Jessie's birthday party nor call for a ride.

My son's best friend lost his home and his brothers when his mom was busted for drugs. Joe's first-grade buddy was shipped to a children's shelter with just the clothes on his back. It was a horrible drug lesson — worse and probably more lasting than any McGruff could teach.

These are hard lessons learned too young. But the lesson that really scares me is this one: My kids have concluded that the kids who don't read well, don't behave or don't have winter jackets are black kids. Because of school busing and the configuration of our neighborhood, my children have come to the mistaken conclusion that black kids are poor and troubled students and that white kids have money and are smart.

Two of the best students in Joe's class are black, but he cannot help but notice first that the largest number of black kids are in the low math class and in trouble with the teachers.

If we lived somewhere else, my children might learn that poor and black are not synonymous, that white kids can be poor and troubled students, too. But we don't. And in any case, it is not the relationship between middle-class whites and poor whites that is central in our country right now. It is the relationship between whites and blacks, and my children are learning the wrong lessons about blacks.

I wish my friend Mike lived in our neighborhood. Mike's family life is just like our own: two kids, a dad who works, coaches kids and fusses over homework, a mom with a part-time job as a teacher, a mortgage, a church. There is a commitment to community service there and a powerful belief in education.

Mike and his family are black. They could teach my children the right lesson: A child's race does not decide how he learns or how he behaves; a child's parents and their economic resources do.

I can't say we will keep our kids in public schools. When the metal detectors go up, we may be gone. My husband and I have talked of moving, but only briefly.

"I don't want to be one of the people that runs away," my husband says, and I know instinctively how costly that statement may be someday.

But it is one of the lessons that I want to make sure my children learn.

# Over the river, through the woods and into the heart

IT IS AUGUST, and the kids will be at Grandma and Grandpa's for a week — a family vacation in the truest sense.

Grandma and Grandpa have time with their grandchildren without the inhibiting middlemen that parents can be. The kids escape the two well-meaning adults who constantly try to mold them into good citizens. And my husband and I glimpse again that gossamer memory of our courtship.

The kids have been going to Pittsburgh every year since they were babies. To a Grandma grateful that her daughter-in-law trusts her with them. From a mother who can't decide if she is more grateful for the break or for the bond that forms between the kids and their grandparents.

By now the routine at Grandma's is set in stone. Joe and Jessie share a double bed in Uncle Danny's old room. There is a TV with a remote control, and, each morning, cartoons are at their fingertips until their stomachs growl.

In the kitchen, Grandma is making whatever they want to eat. The ultimate short-order cook. Sausage and pancakes for breakfast. By noon, there will be kielbasa and sauerkraut or "sewer pipes," Grandma's rigatoni. For dinner, there will be mountains of snow-white mashed potatoes for Joe and all the gravy he can pour.

For a week, my children do nothing. There are no chickens to feed or cows to milk at this Grandma's house. And though their grandparents fret that they should cart them to museums or carnivals or to see the dozen cousins who dot the landscape around Pittsburgh, the kids never want to leave the house. The cocoon of quietude, love and food is what they crave for this week.

Jessie spends her time clomping around in Grandma's high heels and talking her out of another handful of exotic costume jewelry. She raids the fridge for the makings of an ice cream sundae that Grandma buys in anticipation of her arrival. Poor child, she will never find maraschino cherries and marshmallow sauce at home.

Joe makes pilgrimages to the mall with Uncle Kenny for a slice of pizza, a pack of baseball cards or a movie his mother won't let him rent.

Uncle Jeff gives Jessie rides in his red Corvette and sits for tea parties with the ancient dolls Grandma keeps for her.

Grandpa sits still while Jessie styles his hair and peppers him with questions. He chortles softly at everything she does and says. He will say a thousand times before the week is over: "That Jessie is really something."

The children go to Mass with Grandma, and all her Irish friends exclaim, "They are such angels in church" while Grandma smiles as if lighted from above.

At home, things stay where I put them. I fix the screen door — again. For a week at least, it is not punched by a hundred little hands. I clean out closets, sort clothes for school, rent a movie, read a book. I call Grandma's every day, but my kids are too busy doing nothing to talk long.

At the office, my husband, who has too often fled for home after one of my agitated 6 p.m. phone calls, works an unencumbered day and then announces that he is going to meet his wife for dinner. We talk for 10 minutes about world affairs, and then we talk about the kids. We decide we would be workaholics without them.

When we arrive at Grandma and Grandpa's to take the children home, every stitch of clothing is washed and packed, and their faces are fuller, rounder. Grandpa slips them $3 each to spend on junk at "Breezewind" on the Pennsylvania Turnpike.

"They are good kids. You are doing a good job with them," Grandma whispers to me, and nothing she could say pleases me more. But aloud she says, for their benefit, "I holler at them. They don't get away with anything just because they are at Grandma's."

Joe's grin lights up with devilment, and we all laugh. All but Jessie, who turns her head into my chest and weeps softly until Grandma and Grandpa's neighborhood is far behind her.

This has been their ritual for all these summers. We follow it like a script. Someday, they will not want to go to Grandma and Grandpa's. It will be boring or they won't want to leave their friends.

But for now, I think to myself, this is why I had children. So they could go to Grandma and Grandpa's for a week in the summer.

# Middle-school lesson: Idle hands do the devil's work

I AM ON record as not looking forward to the middle-school years.

I have asked every mother I know if there is a way — short of the institutionalization of my children or me — that I can get out of being the parent of a middle-school child, and I have been told repeatedly that there is not.

The years 11 to 13 are not pretty, but there is no way to get to blossoming young adulthood except through them.

My dismay deepened the night of the middle-school open house for incoming sixth-graders. I was looking for an educational vision for children who have mastered reading and writing, and what I got was something that looked like parents' day at summer camp.

The classrooms were lined with collage posters and masks and puppets and dioramas. The ceilings were thick with coat-hanger mobiles. The teachers talked about skits and photographic self-portraits and power tools and sewing machines.

"Oh, God," I murmured. "Cool," said my son.

I went to the open house looking for a summer reading list. I left wondering if craft stores have back-to-school sales.

I went looking for Socratic discussion. I left thinking middle school is some kind of three-year science fair.

I wanted to know if notebooks are graded, if class participation counts, how soon before the midterm the study sheet is distributed. And I saw what looks like three years of shop and art. My son is enthralled, and I am horrified.

Middle school, I thought, is where children get down to the business of reading books. But it is clear that if you can't think in three dimensions and handle a glue gun, you will flunk out.

In language class, they cut out French words and make a collage. In math class, they cut out percent signs and make a collage. In science class, they examine human relationships and make a collage. It is clear that middle school requires a variety of magazine subscriptions.

"I know," said my friend Nancy Anselm, in that consoling voice that wiser mothers often use with the first-timers.

"Middle school is 'Read a book and then bake a cake that explains the book.' My daughter didn't have any real homework for three years.

"The goal is to keep their hands busy and hope they learn something about Egypt while they're at it."

Nancy is an educator as well as a veteran middle-school mother, and I listened as she explained that children of that age are awash in hormones and exhausted from the accelerated pace of their growing.

Like poor Gregor Samsa in Franz Kafka's "The Metamorphosis" (which I am certain they will not read in middle school), they wake up one morning with a body they do not recognize and cannot control.

Likewise, their need to be social is acute, but their ability to be social is inept, so they flop around like landed fish, trying to find their place.

You can't teach these kids anything by standing in front of them and talking.

Administrators say it is important to use a variety of strategies — kinesthetic, visual and auditory — to teach. But my guess is, front-line teachers know that the best way to handle this age is to keep them occupied.

My friend Nancy explained that Maria Montessori, a pioneer in self-directed education, would have agreed.

"Kids are in a fog at that age," Nancy said, paraphrasing Dr. Montessori. "They are out to lunch. It is all going on inside. We can't see it, and we can't force them out of this shell until they are ready. What Maria Montessori said was, while this is going on, we might as well have them doing something practical to prepare them for life. Cooking, child care, the equivalent of shop class.

"It is like occupational therapy. While so much is going on inside of them, keep them busy. And hope they will produce something when they come out of it."

Dr. Montessori would have played to the strengths of this developmental stage, just as middle-school teachers seem to: Kids are so social, they can't shut up. So do plays and skits, work in teams and groups. They are so tactile they can't keep their hands to themselves. So cut, paste, paint, glue and build.

This is cold comfort to the parents who will hear about these projects the night before they are due. But we should have known. These are the children who need seat belts if they are going to finish dinner with us.

What made us think they'd sit still for middle school?

# Be like Cal

I KNOW WE are not supposed to hold sports figures up as role models for our children because, though they may have perfect jump shots, they also have money, women, cars, jewelry and feet of clay.

But I have to say, Cal Ripken's streak of consecutive games played has provided me with more child-rearing leverage than all the threats and bribes in Christendom.

"Cal Ripken didn't dump the last of his milk down the sink, and he's got a $500,000 endorsement contract today because of it."

"Cal Ripken has a Gold Glove, and you can bet he still wears his cup during games. And I'm sure it feels stupid to him, too."

"It's a good thing Cal Ripken didn't get any birthday invitations during the last 2,000 games, or there wouldn't have been any parades for him."

The Streak has received attention beyond Baltimore and beyond all reason. Even a child who collects Magic Cards instead of baseball cards cannot help but know that the Orioles shortstop hasn't taken a day off work since before they were born.

When my 9-year-old daughter, whose sports hero is "Baywatch" Barbie, asked her father why he didn't dye his hair so she could have a young-looking dad, he replied: "Cal Ripken doesn't dye his hair." And she understood.

"Cal Ripken doesn't ask his mother to bring him a soda in the dugout."

"I'm sure Cal Ripken can remember where he put his cleats. After all, his mother didn't wear his, either."

"If Cal Ripken used that tone of voice, he'd have been stuck in his room the last 14 years instead of out playing baseball with his friends."

Charles Barkley, NBA bad boy and superstar, declared a couple of years ago that he didn't want to be a role model for children. (I speak for all mothers when I say, "No problem, Charles.")

"I am not a role model. I'm paid to wreak havoc on a basketball court. It is not my job to raise your kids," Barkley said.

His friend and fellow basketball great Karl Malone responded that this is not an athlete's decision to make. We do not choose to be role models; we are chosen, he said. Our only choice is whether to be good role models or bad ones.

I agree with Barkley that it is unfair of parents to expect athletes to set young people on a path to righteousness. And it is not just because no one can bear up under such incredible scrutiny. Cal Ripken has. In the millions of words written about him this summer, the worst that can be said about him is that he doesn't get much done around the house.

No, the reason athletes cannot be expected to transform young people by their example is that they are too special. They are gifted, truly gifted.

The skills that have taken them to such heights in sports are gifts, and the only credit they can claim is for not wasting them. A child without the right family tree cannot hope to follow in his hero's footsteps. It is sad to watch a child realize that he is not tall, not strong, not fast.

Ripken has such physical gifts. He has displayed them every summer for 14 years. But he has something else, something our kids can have for themselves regardless of their vertical jump or their time in the 40-yard dash or the speed of their fastball.

Among the qualities and character traits we would wish for our children, a strong work ethic is right up there with not hitting your sister and keeping all four legs of the chair on the floor during dinner. And that has been Cal Ripken's gift to us parents. And to our children.

Ripken shows up.

True, he is showing up to play baseball. He is not sitting through algebra or manning a toll booth on the Bay Bridge. And he is rewarded with millions of dollars and the adoration of fans. I'm not sure he would have such sustained joy if he were doing something else.

But my guess is, he would still show up.

Our children can blame us if they don't have the gene pool for professional sports. And I am certain mine will. But Ripken's streak has less to do with his body than his mind and his heart. The guy shows up every day and does his job, and there is nothing genetic about that.

Cal Ripken's professional life has been magical, and I cannot help but wish that for my children as well. But Cal Ripken has taught me a lesson, too. All I should want, or expect, of my children is that they show up. And do their jobs with his combination of earnestness and humility.

# A public debate

THE DAY AFTER my husband and I decided that Jessica would continue to receive a public education, a third-grader in her school was found with marijuana in the pockets of his jeans.

A week after my husband and I decided that our daughter would continue to attend public schools, she came home and asked for the translation of a foul remark made to her by a boy in her fifth-grade class during a soccer game.

Ten days after my husband and I decided that our daughter would continue to attend public schools, Jessie said, in wistfulness, not frustration: "I'd like to go to school with kids like me, kids who like to do their work."

It was only then that my husband and I wondered if we'd made the wrong decision.

We live in the city of Annapolis, and we are old hands in the public-school system there. We continue to volunteer and tutor and fund-raise even though our children, deciding that we are becoming a social handicap, have asked us to back off.

While it isn't Baltimore and it isn't Washington, the public-school system in Annapolis shows many of the symptoms of the diseases that now ravage schools in those cities: the flight of the middle class, disrupted classrooms and battle-weary teachers. Plenty of dope, the occasional weapon, racial tension. Lousy test scores, the promotion of students who are already performing below grade level, dropouts and pregnant girls.

We re-evaluate our decision to send our children to public schools about every 20 minutes, but we have stuck it out, in no small measure because there isn't $20,000 in the family budget for a pair of private-school tuitions.

But I also believe that if we leave public schools, we will have to turn out the lights and lock the door as we go. I believe that if public schools cannot educate our kids, who have no special needs and more parental support than they want, then they can't educate any child. I believe that if we can't stay, there is no reason to ask anyone else to stay.

Choosing public education in our cities is not as simple as walking your first-grader to the doors of the neighborhood school and kissing him goodbye. It is not a default decision, but a conscious one. And the decision does not always turn on money or safety. It would be so much easier for parents if it did. Gangs, knives, guns, bloody fights. These dangers can be seen, and any of us would scrub floors at night for the money to protect a child from them.

The real danger in a public school is less visible and less visibly offensive. But Jessie and her like-minded friends see it.

"I'd like to go to school with kids like me, kids who like to do their work."

Increasingly, public schools are lock-downs for kids who don't want to be there. It is not that they are bored. Bored would be good. Bored would be an improvement. Bored is something teachers can fix.

No, these kids are resentful. They are angry, more so as they move into middle school and high school. They don't think education has any value for them or anyone they know, and they are mad at the teachers who keep preaching that it does.

If my kids asked what practical role prime numbers, invertebrates or dangling participles would have in their daily adult life I would be hard pressed to answer. But kids "who like to do their work" don't have to ask those questions because, intuitively, they know the answer. They see it in the opportunities and the lifestyles around them.

When Jessie said she'd like to go to school with kids like her, she did not mean girls or white girls or middle-class white girls or middle-class white girls who come from intact families and who never back-talk the teacher and always turn in their homework.

She wants to go to school with kids who like to do their work. In an increasingly diverse society, it is the only sameness she requires.

# Kid's room: dig it

WHEN MY CHILDREN were babies, their bedrooms looked as though Penelope Leach and Martha Stewart had been locked inside for a month. Stimulating colors and toys battled with handmade tributes to their birth.

There were primary colors in the wallpaper and black-and-white patterned toys in the crib. There were also cross-stitched samplers and hand-crocheted blankets. Unisex decor and yellow sleepers. Classic children's books lovingly inscribed by me as well as a careful selection of toys designed for tactile stimulation and hand-eye coordination.

Their rooms were a perfect environment for their perfect, new-formed selves, and I could step into those rooms any time and inhale the sweet smell of my babies and see with satisfaction that not a thing was out of place.

That was then. This is now.

Their rooms are no longer a tribute to their birth, but evidence of every battle I have lost since. Their rooms are no longer an environment designed for their development, but evidence of delays in that development. And when I step into those rooms, I inhale mysterious odors, and I see that I have my work cut out for me.

I have tried many times to come to terms with my children's messy rooms, including that time-honored technique of shutting the doors to them, and have settled on a kind of meditative approach. This is my karma, I say as I enter, Zen-like in my tranquillity. I wanted children and these are the two I got and this is the mess they make.

If I am like Siddhartha, I am also like Margaret Mead. I sift through the artifacts of their lives for keys to the society of childhood from which I am banned. What have I learned? Boys and girls are different. The evidence is thrown all over their rooms.

Neither sex would recognize a clothes hanger unless he or she were beaten with one, so there are clothes all over their floors. In a boy's room, however, these clothes are dirty. In a girl's, they have been cast off in fits of indecision.

In my daughter's room, there are pictures of kittens and ballerinas and a collection of stuffed animals, each with a name and a life story. Pierced earrings are scattered like confetti, and hair bobs dot the room with random color. And there are bottles of pastel-colored lotion and bath gel that must be purely ornamental, because they are never used.

In my son's room, there are posters of race cars and soccer players and Cal Ripken and a collection of frogs, some of which are not alive and some of which may not be alive much longer because they have not had a decent meal since they left the rain forest.

While my daughter's room smells like a scratch-and-sniff ad from Cosmopolitan, my son's room smells like a peat bog.

My daughter selected wallpaper with pink flowers. My son selected wallpaper with red stripes.

My daughter has a chalk board on which she writes notes to God. My son has a T-shirt that reads: "Aggressive by nature. Soccer by choice." It is usually dirty and not in the hamper.

Each has piles of books. The difference is, the ones in my daughter's room have been read.

My daughter has set an afternoon tea for dolls in her room. My son has ground nacho chips into the carpet.

My daughter has kept every little thing she has ever been given. In her room there are old birthday cards, handfuls of costume jewelry from Grandma, microscopic Barbie accessories and every souvenir her father has ever brought home from out of town. Each is as precious as a talisman.

There are plenty of mementos in my son's room, too, but that is because he doesn't see the point in throwing anything away if you can just drop it on the floor.

In my daughter's room, there is a pile of papers from which she teaches school to her dolls. In my son's room, those papers are homework assignments he has forgotten to take to school.

This is how I spend those rainy mornings after my children have left for school, sifting through the debris in their rooms for clues to what they like, what they are like.

The bottoms of their closets, under their beds. These squirrels' nests reveal pieces to the puzzle of what is important to my children (Micro Machines or a postcard picture of a baby seal) and what is not (Barbie high heels or church clothes).

And this is how I found a note, yellow with age, that I had written to one of my pack rats years ago. It might have been that this child was too lazy to throw my note away. But I prefer to think that the child had saved it.

It was titled: "10 Things I Like About You."

# Dividing two and getting one

A GREAT MANY social ills have been laid like kindling at the feet of the single parent. Her hands are tied (it is most often a mother) to the stake of public opinion as she waits for someone to strike a match.

Poverty, difficulty at school, early experimentation with sex, drugs and alcohol, petty crime and delinquency. Social scientists confidently predict these things for the children of the woman who tries to raise them without a man around the house. She is blamed for every blemish on society from the disintegration of the family dinner hour to the epidemic of coldhearted teen-age criminals.

When they talk about these women, these parents without partners, I wonder if they are talking about me.

I belong to a shadow demographic group: the de facto single parent.

You won't see our numbers on any U.S. Census. On good days, we would deny our very existence, claiming that we are members of an intact family that tumbles through the week with a healthy mix of love, laughter and careful scheduling.

On bad days, we grumble bitterly that our mate is nothing but a phantom and it is we who face the storm of greedy, needy children.

It is often women who feel thus abandoned by men who cram a 40-hour work week into 60 hours, who commute the distance of a book-on-tape every week, who jump on airplanes, who work shifts, who golf.

But my husband might define himself as a single parent, too, as might the husband of any working mother. He and I tag-team through the week, passing the children like a baton between us. He packs lunches, I do homework. He coaches, I drive.

It has been so long since we had a meal together, he might very well be a vegetarian and I don't know it. He has threatened to dial 900 numbers so he will have another adult to talk to.

My daughter wakes each morning and asks: "Is this a Mommy day or a Daddy day?" I sometimes wonder if her life is much different from the schoolmate who packs a bag for Dad's house every Friday. She has two parents, but she has them serially, not simultaneously.

My children, and a good many children of friends, live with this

Doppler effect. Mom says one thing coming, Dad says another thing going. Our instructions, our disciplining of them, must sound like aphasic speech. The lips of their parents are moving, but the words they hear don't match.

The children adapt, I think. My children and the children of my friends have known nothing else except that Mom leaves before they are fully awake and Dad kisses them while they are sleeping, that Dad muddles through dinner because Mom works nights or that Dad is the weekend coach, but Mom is the homework police.

It is a different matter for the parents, though. We didn't get married so we could ride in separate cars to the same pizza parlor or soccer game. We didn't get married so we could leave notes on doors or messages on answering machines. We didn't get married so we could each have a cell phone. We did not expect to argue about whose work schedule is more critical.

We didn't get married so we could be single parents.

But we are. Either Dad is out slaying the beast while Mom stays home and grinds the corn, or Mom and Dad are both out trying to slay a beast large enough to feed the kids, who wear keys to the cave around their necks.

We are all working very hard for the family, but while we are thus occupied, the family evaporates.

My husband talks sometimes about giving it all up and "living Amish," as he calls it. He is taken by the glimpses he has had of the lives of these simple people, and he would like that life for us: spending the day with the children in an ambitious version of yardwork, going to bed with the sun and rising at dawn to the smell of my baked ham and homemade pies.

Reincarnation or remarriage is his only path to that world, but he has tapped into a national longing for a less complicated life. Journalists and pollsters have discovered a deep and troubling dissatisfaction with our work-and-spend treadmill, and, though people are uncertain how to accomplish it, many express a willingness to reduce significantly their standard of living if it would mean a simpler life.

It is one of the ironies of all of this that though it most often takes two people to keep the American family solvent, we feel that we are doing it alone.

# Girl power

IF YOU KNEW Hannah like we know Hannah, you wouldn't be surprised to hear that the principal called. Hannah is 7 years old, shaped like a bullet, and moving through life like one.

Compactly and powerfully built, with a gravelly, grown-up voice and a determined manner, Hannah takes no prisoners, gives no quarter, suffers no fools.

If you knew Hannah like we know Hannah, you'd never wonder whether Hannah will make a place for herself in this world.

You would also not be surprised to learn that the principal called Hannah's parents and reported, in a very nice way, that Hannah had depantsed a little boy during recess and perhaps they should all meet and talk.

"We never got the full story," said Hannah's father, his voice perpetually weary from being Hannah's father. "Was it a tug or full down to the ankles?

"But to the principal's credit, she just suggested that we have a talk with Hannah and did not make this a constitutional question."

That's good, because Hannah's father had plenty of questions of his own.

"At first I thought, 'Well, this is just another childhood thing.' Then I thought, 'No. Hannah did this to embarrass me. This is directed at me. This is about me.'

"Things like this should never involve our own children. It should just involve other people's children, so we can comment on it."

Everyone did, of course. Hannah's father is a very funny guy, and his retelling of Hannah's adventures always draws a crowd.

"If this was someone else's child, I'd be laughing, too. But no one had any good advice. You could see they were all glad it wasn't their kid."

Hannah's father and mother thought hard about how to respond. That was their first mistake. "Do we say nothing, cut off her allowance, put her on bread and water for a month, go to the library and check out a book on Freud?

"Whenever parents worry about whether they are doing the right thing, you can be pretty sure they are not doing the right thing. If you have to think about it, that's the first sign that you are going to do the wrong thing."

Hannah's father says he views child-rearing questions like this — what do you do if your daughter pulls down a boy's pants on the playground — as the adult version of the Scholastic Assessment Test, a kind of parental SAT.

"Raising kids is all multiple choice, and they tell you before you take the SATs: DON'T GUESS. Don't ever guess. You will be penalized for guessing. It will count against you if you guess.

"I am guessing here. I am probably guessing wrong and, just like I did on my SATs, I am going to score, like, 480 out of a possible 1,600."

The first impulse Hannah's father had was to let the children resolve it with the kind of "Lord of the Flies" rough justice that operates on playgrounds.

"If you get out of their way, kids take care of their own affairs. They punish their own. They have their own little playground judicial system.

"But after what happened in North Carolina, with the first-grader who kissed the girl and was accused of sexual harassment, I felt like I had to file a friend-of-the-court brief. There is a serious side to this.

"We told Hannah that you never embarrass another child.

"We kind of left the whole Constitution out of it. No Aesop's fables, no quotations from the Bible.

"We just said that she would not have liked it if he had done that to her. That there was no 'coolness quotient' in this for her."

Joe thought it was cool.

"Hannah flagged a kid on the playground?" said my middle-school son as he laughed with delight.

Joe has known Hannah since she was a baby, and has always had a respect for her that he accords no other girls. It is born, I suspect, of a healthy fear.

"Way to go, Hannah," crowed Joe. "Did she, like, get his pants all the way down, or just flag his boxers?"

"That's not clear," I said to Joe, with the irritation in my voice that I knew was appropriate to show.

"And that's not the right response. We're not supposed to cheer from the sidelines while one child humiliates another."

But I was. My secret voice was hooting, "Way to go, Hannah."

I love gumption in a girl, even as I recognize my double standard is wrong. It is the flip side of the kind of permission-to-abuse that has been the subtext of the treatment of little girls and women for generations.

I know that if a little boy had pulled down Hannah's pants on the playground — or my own daughter's — I would have demanded chemical castration, and I would have administered it myself. When my feminist politics mix with my maternal instincts, I can be ferocious and unreasonable.

I know this is not right thinking for the new egalitarian world order, but I can't quash my enthusiasm for the spirit I see in Hannah. OK, OK. It's misdirected at the moment, but she is only 7 years old.

It is a fine line we walk as we try to teach our daughters to take the reins of the world, not a back seat. That in order to wear the pants in town, you don't have to pull someone else's off.

What did Hannah's father do?

"We told her to write him a letter of apology. It said, 'I'm sorry.' That's about as much as she could spell. She put some stickers in the envelope for him.

"She put $2 in the card, too, but I took the money out. I tried to explain to Hannah that really wasn't part of the message we wanted to send."

# Telling it like it is

I AM ENGAGED in an exhaustive, and exhausting, debate on the best way to raise children, but unfortunately it is not with Penelope Leach, my husband or even my mother.

It is with my children.

I am not sure exactly when this happened, and indeed it might have been just a slow loosening of my grip on the reins of power, but my children have come to believe that they should be equal partners in the business of bringing them up.

And for a while I have indulged them. For the sake of those precious lines of communication we keep hearing about, for the sake of their self-esteem, I have listened to their complaints and criticism and their cries of unfairness.

During each argument, I have carefully restated their concerns in a nonjudgmental way to let them know that I have heard them and that I accept them for who they are.

(As an aside, I should say that this approach, called "active listening" in Parent Effectiveness Training, did not work well. After about three minutes of my repeating everything he said, my son exploded in frustration. "Is there an echo in here, or are you just deaf?")

As part of this child-rearing debate with my children, I have been unfavorably compared to every other mother on the planet — and to their father, who brings candy home from his office and presents home from business trips — but I have been patient.

No more.

I have had it.

When my son said, "Even Bill Clinton says children should be able to divorce their parents," something like a grenade went off inside my head, and I have been barking at my children like an angry dog since.

When my 11-year-old son demanded, yet again, to be allowed to rent violent video games and R-rated movies like absolutely everyone else he knows, I dispensed with my usual speech — the one about his being a beautiful flower and my need to protect him from an early frost.

Instead, I said: "Forget it. This is not a discussion. There is no debate. I don't want to hear your side of this, because I don't care what you think.

"These are the facts: I'm the one with the driver's license and the video card. And until you have your own apartment with your own television, you're trapped inside my value system.

"End of discussion."

When both children whined — yet again — that they did not want to go to Sunday school, that it is boring and their lives are already too busy and why couldn't they watch cartoons on Sunday morning, I dispensed with my usual speech about how an hour of their time is not too much for God to ask considering all that he has done for them, especially in the worldly possessions category.

Instead, I said: "Forget it. You skip school, they only keep you back a year. You skip Sunday school, you go to hell. Now get your books and get in the car."

When the bickering between them reached a crescendo and I heard a sharp slap followed by the wailing of my 9-year-old daughter, I dispensed with my usual speeches. The one to my daughter about how when her father and I are gone, she and her brother will have only each other and she needs to find a way to be friends with him. And the one to my son about how if he continues to bully his sister, she will grow up to expect such abuse from a man and marry badly.

Instead, I told my daughter to stop being the "Wimp of the Western World" and to bite her brother if she could think of no other way to drive him away.

My son howled at the unfairness of my suggestion, said it was child abuse and threatened to call 911. (Have you noticed? Children are always threatening to call 911.)

"Go ahead," I said smugly. "What do you think will happen? Do you think they will take me away in cuffs? That's not the way it works, pal. They remove the child from the dangerous domestic environment.

"That means you'll be hauled off to a foster home, where you will sleep in a room with nine other boys, eight of whom wet the bed.

"And me? I'll be at the movies."

As you can see, the waters have crested in my house. I am done listening to the demands of children on how they would like to be raised. This child-rearing by committee is not working, especially when two members of the committee are children.

I keep my own counsel now, and my children are baffled by the new me. You can imagine their surprise when, after they suggested that they would live in their own rooms after college so they could save money to buy cars and go to the mall, I did not respond with a group hug.

"Oh, didn't I tell you? Your father and I are selling the house as soon as you two leave for college. We are going to buy a one-bedroom condo, and we won't even have a sleep sofa."

"You're just kidding, right, Mom?' Joe asked anxiously. "This is all just a joke, right?"

I answered with a smile, and it was inscrutable.

# Chapter 5

*My fellow*
**Mothers**

# My co-authors

SELF-ESTEEM IS A little tough to come by these days, unless of course you are a child and your parents have heard how important it is to your success in life and you get praised for everything from straight A's to not tripping over cracks in the sidewalk.

If you are a mom, you don't have much self-esteem. I don't know exactly when it happens, but at some point you lose the expectation that really special things will happen for you — and you focus on making them happen for your children. Their little successes thrill you like your successes never did.

But then, after 20 years in this business, I got my picture in the paper for something other than an untimely death. I became a columnist, and I turned to the bosom of my family for praise and reinforcement. Wrong.

What I got was painful honesty. They were honest, and it was painful for me.

To begin, my mother did not respond as I might have wished. Nothing new there. When has your mother ever given you the credit you deserve?

"Mom, great news," I began, and explained how I had resurrected my career.

"Oh, my. I thought you were going to tell me something about Danny's new baby," she said, sounding disappointed that this wasn't news about my new niece.

When I explained that I thought getting a column was a pretty big deal, she said: "Well, dear. You know I always like hearing about your little job."

All four of Jean Reimer's daughters have little jobs. Cynthia is a little market researcher, Ellen is a little office manager, Elizabeth is a little nurse. We all feel like we work in Munchkinland.

OK. Next stop, my husband.

"That's great, honey, but here's some advice," he said, and he is in this business, so I listened.

"Pick a picture and stick with it. Don't change it every three months, or they will think you're unstable."

My daughter had trouble with the picture thing, too. But she was kind. Dear Jessie, she is always looking out for my looks. I think she thinks I'm shabby.

"Mom," she said, and she put her hand reassuringly on my arm, "I don't think you will like this new job. I saw the pictures. Everyone's face is gray and their hair is black."

And leave it to my son, Joe, to find my darkest heart.

"Dad," he said when told the news, "how does Mom know she's ever going to have another good idea?"

And so, it was up to my women friends to cheer me, arriving at my home that first Tuesday morning with flowers, gifts, champagne and coffee cake.

They treated me like lifers might treat a fellow prisoner who's been paroled from The Big House.

"I feel like this is happening to me," said Paula, who started a scrapbook for me. Nancy and Linda brought flowers. Diana gave me a journal for whatever thoughts I don't exploit in this space. Betsy, the lawyer, composed a biting and hysterically funny "waiver and release" absolving me of any wrongdoing when and if I expose my friends' private lives in the name of this job. Peg and Nan and a pitcher of margaritas helped write it, and they all signed it.

They autographed a baseball in memory of my sportswriting days. "Paul's mother," read one signature — the name my children gave one friend years ago.

These are friends born of car-pooling convenience, friends made as a result of choices made by my children. Our kids go to the same school or they are on the same teams or they're friends.

But chance was never so good to so many. These are women who are there for me, and for each other, every day. Something much stronger than the on-again, off-again nature of children's friendships has bound us together.

Some are stay-at-home moms — the safety net for all of us who work. They are there when school closes early for snow, there when your child gets sick during math, there when your son needs stitches in a playground injury and you are an hour away.

And some are working moms — women who will watch your children on their precious days off. And who share their tearful view from the center of a chaotic life, helping you to know that somebody may indeed have it worse than you.

They are the women your kids go to without fear or shyness. Women your children treat better than they treat you. Women who know your kids best — and like them anyway.

These are the women who have been saying for years, "You know, you really ought to write this stuff down."

# Board of advisers

IT HAS BEEN 30 years since my mother had a young child to raise, and when she looks at me across the gulf of experiences those years represent, she cannot relate to the demands of my motherhood.

It exhausts her just to hear about the running around I do, to dance lessons, soccer games, art classes, swim practices. There was no money for those things when my sisters and I were young and — more important — there was no pressure to do them. No one else was doing them either.

When I was writing big checks to pay for my children's fancy-schmancy preschool education, my mother pointed out that when I was 5 years old, kindergarten was optional. The bus fare of $5 was a luxury, she told me, and so I did not go. And, she noted, not only did I learn to cut and paste and socialize just fine, but I also went to college and found a decent job.

When she hears me talk about school board meetings and redistricting hearings, about the merits of whole language learning or about homogeneous vs. heterogeneous grouping, she is lost. My husband spends more time volunteering at my children's school in a single year than my mother — and perhaps yours — spent during my entire educational life. I think I recall seeing her there for one Hot Dog Day.

And, so, when I turn tearfully to my mother with a sad tale about my crazy life, she cannot say to me, as she often did when I was sick, "I know sweetheart — me, too."

But I have filled the void where my mother's words of wisdom might be with a kind of advisory panel — a group of women whose children are my children's ages and older.

As their kids pass through different phases, different stages, as they trot out different idiosyncrasies to drive their parents mad, I watch and listen. I am careful to see how these mothers respond. I have learned that, too soon, I will go through the same trials. My friends are my road maps through life.

It was not always so. I can still hear myself say as I watched my friends raise their very young children: "Humpf. My kids will never drink soda, eat chocolate or watch commercial television. I will never use food as a reward. I will never bribe my kids with some stupid purchase just to get them to cooperate. I will never negotiate with them..." Should I go on, or do you hear the same voice in your memory?

Each vow I took was quickly broken. The reality of raising children erased the absolutes I had established. I thought I would learn from my friends' mistakes. But what I learned was what the future held for me.

It can be a fearful picture. "Put your feet up," a friend told me, and she laughed a haunted laugh. "Nine-year-old boys are easy. Piece of cake. Wait until puberty hits. Then you just buckle your chin strap and hold on."

"Wait until she's 12 or 13," another friend said about my loving daughter. "She's going to hate you."

I am fearful of what they describe, because I know there is truth in what they say. Their own lives have predicted my future so often that I have learned to hold my arrogant tongue, watch and learn.

I remember thinking, when a dear friend started hauling her daughter an hour away for voice lessons: "She's nuts. No children's theater experience is worth this kind of trouble and expense." Now, my own daughter wants that theater experience, and Silver Spring does not seem so far away.

I remember thinking when she let her son walk to the comic-book store each Friday to spend his allowance: "Not my son. He's going to be reading junior novelizations." But when my own reluctant reader asked if he could do a book report on a comic-book version of Cal Ripken's life, I was delighted. "At least he's reading," I told myself.

Now, her son is a senior, and he is known as the only kid in the history of the school to have done all the reading in Advanced Placement History. I am watching, I told my friend, and hoping the pattern holds.

And so, as my kids snack on Yoo-hoos and microwave french fries and watch some cartoon show I abhor, as we argue about homework and whether it is acceptable to call someone a butthead, I watch and listen as my friends face the deadly issues of adolescence: drinking, drugs and sex. Here's hoping they get through it OK. Then perhaps I will, too.

# Pulling up an anchor

NAN HAS GONE back to work. Her oldest will soon go to college and her youngest can keep track of a house key, so it is time.

And while the three boys she has been at home with for 15 years have not missed a beat since she returned to teaching, Nan's friends may never get over the loss.

She will not be there for a cup of coffee after the kids leave for school — her front porch was just the place to postpone the start of your day. And though she will be home after school (as in: "Kids, if Mommy doesn't get home in time, just go to Nan's"), when a woman works, her friends are timid about adding to her burdens. A rambunctious group of second- and third-graders at a nearby school will have the benefit of Nan's firm hand and cheerful voice, but that is precisely what the children in our school will lose.

Nan will not be there to tutor the children who can't quite keep up, or to make 500 star cookies at the conclusion of the "Math Superstars" program that will now have to be run by someone else. Nan will not be there on school field trips to make sure your child neither gets lost nor displays his worst manners. She will no longer be a "Picture Person," and introduce grade-schoolers to great works of art. And she won't be there to teach the kindergartners about Hanukkah.

(At a volunteer luncheon not long ago, she was given a certificate for more than 1,000 hours. "I'm sure it was a math error," she said to those who could not conceive of those 1,000 hours.)

And she will not be there for my daughter, Jessie, who, fearing the boys on the playground, would "get sick" just before recess and tell the school secretary — whether it was true or not — "My mom isn't home today. Just call Nan."

I would find her at Nan's, sipping tea and watching "Pollyanna" from a couch made up like a bed. At Nan's, Jessie had found refuge from the boys and the stern questions of her mother.

None of us knows the price the world pays for working mothers until the bill comes due to us, until the cost is personal. Those of us who depend on women such as Nan to be there when we are not — in school and at home — feel as if we are working without a safety net when they return to the work force. Though the jury may still be out on the impact of day care on children, the impact of working mothers on their friends is real and calculable.

Nan is paying a price, too, and it is a familiar one to women who work. When she was childless, she taught in the toughest schools, committed herself to the kids who needed her most. But those needy kids and the public school system would leave nothing in her for her own children. The choice she made — limited hours at a tiny private school full of students as bright as new pennies — is the kind of choice working mothers often make. Things such as social conscience, ladder-climbing, big money or long hours often take a back seat to flexibility.

So, Nan cleaned out all her closets, read up on the educational wheels reinvented in the past decade, bought bright new things for her bulletin boards and a couple of new dresses.

She marked, "Please do not send this month's selection" on her Book-of-the-Month Club invoice and sighed one last time at all the tasks that will not get done this school year, all the precious time with books, women friends and other people's children that she will not have.

She told her youngest that if she is not home after school, he may have to go to a friend's house. And then Nan returned to work.

It might not be long before my other friends go, too. The president of the Parent-Teacher Organization had to resign because she saw tuition bills looming and returned to work. When the oldest gets close to college, when the youngest becomes self-sufficient, the pressure increases on stay-at-home moms to earn a paycheck. The volunteer work force, the support system for the schools and for those of us who work, is dwindling.

As Nan's friends, we talked once about pooling our resources and paying her to stay home, to be there for us, for our kids, for our school.

But we decided we could never pay her enough to do what she has always done for free.

# Aunt colony

BY THE TIME we left, my own children were calling me "Aunt Susan."

By the end of a month among my three sisters, even they were calling me "Aunt Susan."

In fact, all four of us were wearing grooves in that courtesy title, referring to each other as Aunt This and Aunt That, and using it even to name ourselves in that odd third-person way mothers have of speaking to their children.

"Aunt Susan is on the phone right now," I would say to my daughter. "Please don't interrupt."

For four surreal weeks of illness and grief, my children and I lived among my sisters and all the cousins. We slept in different guest rooms and on different family-room floors, on roll-out sofas and in sleeping bags, as we shifted our base of operations to be nearer one sickbed or another, one funeral home or another.

We buried my mother and my husband's father and a dear friend, staying in Pittsburgh until my children used up all their tears and all their dress clothes and the smell of flowers made us feel sick.

And, I am not ashamed to say, having a wonderful time.

For a month, I lived among my sisters' families, all tangled up in their daily routines, their marriages and their kids.

And for a month, they were all tangled up in mine.

We saw each other without make-up and without pretense. No holiday dresses and no best behavior. No glowing summary of life shared quickly over a long-distance telephone line.

We saw each other's good days and bad days, and we saw them not from a safe distance but from the inside. We astonished each other with strength and forgave each other's weaknesses.

And we did each other's laundry and scolded each other's children.

"My goal," said Aunt Ellen to my Joseph, "is to send you home grateful that Aunt Susan is your mother."

"There are only two ways to deal with Aunt Cynthia," I said to her brooding son, Stephen, "agree with her or get out of her way. Trust me, I know."

We were gentle to each other's husbands, recognizing the whirlwind we reap when the four of us are together, and we fed each other's families. I trotted out all six of my recipes, and I left everyone believing that I am a wonderful cook.

By the end of a month, callers could not tell which one of us answered the phone because we had begun to sound alike. Children did not know whether they heard an aunt they must answer or a mother they could ignore.

"I think I found all your underwear," my husband said into the receiver. "I'll bring it to you when I come out."

"Ummmm, I don't think you've got the right one," said my sister.

I cleaned out one sister's kitchen cabinets and another's garage. I folded one sister's wash and, because I did, bought her husband new boxers for his birthday.

One niece entertained my grieving daughter with paper dolls while I took another one back-to-school shopping.

"You're going to hate this," my niece warned. "My mother is always really mad at me by the end." But because she was my sister's picky child, I was not.

The nephew whose politics disappoint me and whose argumentative nature irritates me was also the one to tell me in a private moment that he admired my guts.

The quiet boy who is so often lost in the cacophony of family holidays lingered without speaking in my embrace for the longest time one sad afternoon.

Aunt Liz's son Rudi, collecting litter at 6 a.m. in the parking lot of the driving range where he worked this summer, recognized two of his aunts in a car that pulled up next to him.

And they recognized chew tobacco behind his lower lip.

Aunt Cynthia and I sent a torrent of scolding out the car window that, we are sure, caused the boy to wonder if he was under surveillance.

"Mom," my son asked, "are you going to use all Aunt Ellen's rules when we get home, or is it just because we are at her house?"

"Joe, you're not going to like the answer," I said. "My fondest wish is to be more like Aunt Ellen."

I have a new curling iron because of Aunt Ellen, she has a new lettuce spinner because of me. My nephew wants a Playstation. My daughter wants a kitten and pantyhose.

For a month, my sisters and I lived in a twilight of reunion and loss, laughing through tears at a slumber party from hell. We shared clothes, jewelry, make-up, recipes, sex stories, child-rearing strategies and memories so different that we began to wonder if we might not have grown up with three other women.

Now, my children and I are back home in Maryland, and we have picked up our busy lives as if this sad summer had never happened.

And my sisters are drifting back into the mists of Pittsburgh and their own chaotic schedules. When I reach out for them, I am hearing answering machines, as I know they are when they reach out for me. I miss them.

I left home years ago to become one instead of one of four. I wanted to be an adult instead of the oldest daughter.

I do not regret that leave-taking. But I regret the one I made at the end of a month among my sisters.

# Visiting at a sisterly pace

SHE HAS COME to visit me just about every year for 17 years, but for 16 of them we have done Washington the way you do Washington when friends and relatives visit with children. The National Zoo. The Air and Space Museum. The frantic search for bathrooms and food vendors.

This time, she came without children, and we did Washington the way two women would do Washington. Museums, art galleries. Tea. Lingering. Laughing.

She left her home in Pittsburgh papered with lists. The matrix of the activities of four children cross-referenced.

"My oldest said, after rolling his eyes at my fifth set of reminders, 'Mom, you know this place runs itself,'" Cynthia said. "I almost smacked him. Instead, I'm having that chiseled in stone."

We met for breakfast at the Old Ebbitt Grill near the White House and the words poured out of us like steaming coffee. We have talked long and often over the years, but always within earshot of our children. The result is we have never completed a thought, must less exhausted a topic.

I would like to say that we talked politics and world affairs — something suitable for a power breakfast in the nation's capital. But I can only say that we did not talk about our children. Or our husbands. Or our mother. We talked of hemlines and clothing labels and then the waiter brought more hot water for our tea and we talked of movies and books.

"I wanted to see what women wear here," she said, gazing around the dim, whispery room at the Old Ebbitt. "Hats. I have seen all these hats. I didn't imagine anyone wore hats except on Easter Sunday."

We toured the White House, and I told her of an interview I did there with a "senior domestic policy adviser." I told her that I spilled coffee all over the blue suit I'd worn to look the part, and she laughed that laugh she has that makes me feel like I am so funny. The miles between her kitchen table and my job melted away.

Then we did the galleries. Wore the headphones. Listened to the curator tours. We were lost in learning things we knew we did not need to know, but loving the process. Remembering when learning was something we did, instead of something we make sure children do.

"No one is ever going to ask me about the first 100 years of photography unless they need it for a school report," she said.

She was impressed, she said, with all the public buildings in Washington and how beautifully they were maintained. "My tax dollars at work," said this Republican woman with a shrug of resignation. "I understand it better now. I want there to be a security guard beside Salvador Dali's 'Last Supper.' "

But the street people upset her. There are plenty in Pittsburgh, and she has parceled out dollar bills all over downtown at the behest of her tearful children. But she did not expect to see them sleeping in the lobby of the Kennedy Center. She could not resolve the incongruity.

She asked — delicately, the way you might ask the maitre d' where the restrooms are — why so few people in Washington spoke English. She wondered why all the street vendors sold ties.

I thought the Metro might eat her alive. The unspoken courtesy of leaving the left lane on the escalator open for those who want to climb quickly almost got her trampled. This is a woman who gets vertigo getting up from the dinner table. She would never race up an escalator that looks like it is climbing to the clouds.

Besides, we are used to a different kind of hurrying. Not the kind with a briefcase in your hand — the kind where you are getting everybody else out the door in the morning.

We took a cab to the Four Seasons Hotel in Georgetown for afternoon tea, and the little, old driver played classical music on the car radio. "I like to play nice music for my ladies," he said. Cynthia and I were quiet. Lost in thought.

We drank port, ate finger sandwiches and sipped tea while a handsome man in a tuxedo played a Steinway nearby. There was no one with us who would soon get bored, soon crane his head for a waiter and a check.

We lingered as the soft cushions of the terrace garden couches drew our tired bodies deeper. Contented, we seemed to be all talked out. Funny, it only took 17 years.

My eyes burned when we said goodbye. "When you come again," I said, "we'll do the zoo and the Air and Space Museum."

And she laughed that laugh she has that makes me feel like I am so funny.

# Hard-won freedom

"I AM NOT a feminist," she said. "I don't believe in feminism."
She said it as if she didn't need to be a feminist. As if it wasn't relevant anymore. As if she would get by on her own merit. She is a college student, and she said the feminists on her campus offended her. Their ideas offended her. And she said it as if feminism means hating men, forswearing marriage and children, behaving like a battle ax in public.

I had heard it before from young women, this notion that you don't have to be a feminist to succeed. That sexism, like communism, had long ago fallen of its own weight. That it had all been taken care of.

Hey, I want to tell them, belong or don't. Sign up and call yourself a feminist or go it alone. But don't for one minute think that your sex doesn't matter anymore.

When you applied to college, I wanted to tell her, somebody put your application in the pile marked "women." And when someone gives you a job, it will be because you are a woman.

Either your employer needs a woman to spruce up his affirmative action image, or he has discovered that women often outwork men in their attempt to stay even with them, and he doesn't mind reaping the benefits of that. But he is hiring you because you are a woman.

He will probably also hire you because of your looks. Pretty and thin matters. For some men, it doesn't matter a great deal. For other men employers, it is all that matters. But it matters. When they think about hiring you, one of the things men think about is whether they would mind having you around to look at.

Once you are hired, you will undoubtedly earn less money than a man for all or part of your work life. Perhaps you are trapped in fields such as teaching, banking and insurance, where women are concentrated but powerless and paid less as a result. Perhaps you are juggling the demands of home and work and aren't free to make the commitments that will earn you more. Or perhaps your employer simply thinks he can hire you for less than he has to pay a man. But you will earn less, and it will be because you are a woman.

Sometime, some man in your workplace will make a pass at you. It may be a vague comment that you fear you might be misinterpreting. Or some guy might pin you against the wall in the elevator. But sometime during your work life, it will happen. Think about it now, because how you respond will affect your future. Ask Navy Lt. Paula Coughlin, who blew the whistle on the boys at the Tailhook convention.

If you are lucky, the men you work with will treat you in a professional manner. They might fear the consequences of not doing so, or they might consider themselves too cool, too correct to react to you in any other way. Or they might decide you have earned that kind of treatment. But you are a woman, and men know the world is watching how they behave toward you.

If you are not so lucky, the men you work for will try to derail your career. They might not promote you, or give you the assignments or projects you need to succeed. They might be threatened by you or think you can't do the job or they might pass over you without giving it a thought. Simply because you are a woman.

I know this all sounds bitter and negative. But these are the rules of the game. If you think that you are just a walking academic record or a breathing job history, unaffected by your sex or your looks, you are wrong.

This may not be a big factor in your life. But it will never not be a factor. It is not a level playing field for women. There are advantages and disadvantages, but sex is never a neutral issue.

Even if you choose to stay home and raise your children, it is a choice that is yours because society believes you are better equipped to do it and has made some effort, however small, to support that decision.

And so it infuriates me when the next generation of women declares that they are not feminists. Being a feminist isn't about making the workplace an armed camp or hating men or being a lesbian or discarding marriage or child-rearing.

It is about choices and the freedom to make those choices. Listen to the women who have gone before you; they know. If you think for one minute that the fact that you are a woman isn't a factor in the choices you are allowed to make, you are wrong.

# Choosing your friends

THEY SAY THAT you cannot choose your family, but my children have done a pretty good job.

We live far from our relatives, but Joe and Jessie have extended our family through their choice of friends. The parents of their playmates are our helpmates.

The fabric of life may be strained by Mom's job and Dad's commute, but my children have mended those weak spots with a patchwork of kids and their moms, kids and their dads. More than friends, closer than cousins, we parents of these children have bonded. We do more than depend on each other in emergencies. We could not survive, not happily anyway, without each other. With the parents too busy, the children have redefined community.

Everywhere I look in my neighborhood, I see the pattern repeated: symbiotic relationships between families that extend beyond car pooling. Adults thrown together by the choices their children make on the playground grow to be connected first by convenience and then by a peculiar brand of intimacy.

We scold each other's children with a dragon's tongue, and we nurse them with a pretty good imitation of their mother's touch. Each husband will call the wives of the others for help without hesitation or embarrassment — the surest test of the co-dependency of families.

This is what communities were like in simpler times. When you could count on any neighborhood mother to tell on you or feed you dinner. Where children were always safe because everyone felt responsible for everyone else, to everyone else.

It is done on a much smaller scale now, just two or three families all tangled up in each other's lives instead of entire city blocks, entire suburban cul-de-sacs. Kid-sized, which makes sense because the kids make the choices.

For us, it is Joe and Susan and their kids, Paul and Joanna. We are a matched set. Two women who love movies, books and conversation. Two men who lift their dialogue from the sports pages. Two boys who have wrestled like puppies since preschool, but never fought. Two girls who could not speak when they met, but who now share the snippy talk and endless chatter of 8-year-old teen-agers.

We began as a car pool. I think every mother's friendships begin that way. Now, we write each other's work schedules on our calendars. Our lives are connected at so many points, it would be simpler to live in the same house. But it would be more than convenient. It would be a warm, centered kind of life.

I don't know. Maybe we would hate each other after a long weekend. After all, hell is other people's children. The little bit of air that exists in our lives now may be what freshens this relationship.

Susan often feeds my husband and children when I am gone. And I do the same for Joe and the kids when she is working. I know Joanna won't eat noodles with sauce. Susan knows my son won't eat fruit. Paul loves my grilled cheeses.

Susan will watch my children on her precious days off. I have watched Paul while my own were at school. "She likes me, Mom," Paul says. She is incredulous. He is proud.

Susan bakes with my daughter and sews dress-up clothes. Her husband will take the kids to any sporting event; mine paints T-shirts with the girls at the kitchen table. Both men have coached the other's children, and found nice things to say, to the mothers, anyway.

Susan and I have shared tears. Joe chases the gloom from Gary with his relentless cheerfulness. Each husband has confessed, in bits and pieces, the admiration he holds for his wife to the wife of his friend. The fact that Susan and I tell each other what our husbands cannot seem to say to us has carried each of us over rough spots in our marriages.

The mesh is not always so smooth. I long for an afternoon with one woman friend, but our children grate on each other. I struggled toward friendship with the mothers of my son's best friends, and only recently have felt the kinship the boys have known for years. My daughter's best friend has moved, and I feel the loss of the mother as keenly as Jessie does the child. And I did not know it until the moving van arrived.

My husband and I are too often exhausted by the pace of a two-career life, with just enough energy left to worry about the job we are doing raising our kids. There is so little time left for friendships that we could easily feel lonely and isolated.

It is a good thing that Joe and Jessie have made our friends for us.

# Baby love

THERE HAS BEEN an unexpected bonus in my daughter's piano lessons — and her name is Katie. She is the 18-month-old daughter of the piano teacher, and after each lesson, I get to hold Katie under the pretense of saying goodbye.

It is a very long goodbye, for Katie has leaped from the imagination of a doll maker. Crystal blue eyes as round and big as quarters. Tiny lips pressed into a bow by her puffy, pillowy cheeks. And when I hold her, Katie melts into my shoulder as if she wants to nap there.

Katie drives away all reason, and I am intoxicated with her, with the idea of her. With the idea of having a third child.

It is unlikely — my husband says that though he can see himself as a 55-year-old baseball coach, he can't see me as a 55-year-old PTA mom — but I am preoccupied with the romantic notion of one more baby.

It is unreasonable to shatter the perfect symmetry of a two-parent-two-child family, I know. ("Man-to-man coverage," explains my husband, the sportswriter. "Nobody escapes for a touchdown.") We have one of each sex and both arrived safely and it is folly to tempt fate.

They are older now, and life is manageable, the way it would not be with a new baby. Our daily routines would become daily productions if the number of kids outnumbered the number of adults.

With two children, I can fake normal life. But with three, I'd have to face the fact that I'd be out of action for at least six years. I can't imagine crossing the street with three kids, let alone getting out the door in the morning for work.

But I have only to watch the way the soccer mothers rushed to the woman holding the newborn to know that I am not the only 40-year-old still clinging to this vision of herself as a woman young enough still to have children.

We would all protest that we would not go back to night feedings and diapers for love or money, but when we are battling adolescents who tell us to get out of their lives twice a day, it would be lovely to have somebody to love — us. Again. For a while longer.

The statistics weigh heavily against this sentimental daydream.

When you are thinking about a third child, you see large families

137

everywhere, but the truth is, it is a cottage industry, not a national trend. The Department of Fertility Statistics at the Bureau of the Census says the American family is shrinking. In just one generation, the average number of children per couple has dropped from three to under two (1.8).

In 1970, according to the Census Bureau, 17 percent of the nation's households had three or more children. In 1992, just 7 percent were that large.

While large families tend to be two-parent families, they are less likely to be two-income families. Census statistics show that 68 percent of married women with one child are in the labor force, compared with 64 percent of married women with two children and 55 percent of married women with three or more.

When women are surveyed, they list stress and financial concerns as the most important reasons why they do not have a third child, while affordability and the ability to give each child some attention are the two biggest reasons given for small family size.

We are shrinking our families to a size we can cope with, a size we can pay for. But that does nothing to extinguish the longings.

Most of us came from larger families, and there is an almost primal need to match the size of our family of origin. But we are also the children of "zero population growth" and more than two children does not seem to us like a responsible act.

And it would not be greeted favorably. If you are pregnant for the third time, people feel free to ask, "Why?" "Was this planned?" "Are you happy about this?"

Often a third child is conceived at the time when the second child enters school. When the woman is free to devote more time to a career and does not, unkind observers will suggest that she is afraid of an existence defined by something other than child-rearing.

The mothers I know might protest that they are content to hand the delightful Katies of the world back to their mothers. That babies are sweetest when they are not your own.

But I suspect there is more of this ambivalence in these women than they are likely to admit.

If they held Katie, I bet they would linger. And daydream.

# May fair

MAY IS THE cruelest month.

T. S. Eliot said that about April, but he was talking about lilacs, not children. If he had had children, he would have known May is the cruelest month.

May is the month of deadlines, recitals, graduations, picnics, championships and rain dates. The month when sports coaches, ballet mistresses, schoolteachers and parents lunge toward summer, dragging bewildered and uncooperative children with them.

In May, our lives read like the epitaph to Ben Gazzara's "Run for Your Life." Twenty years of living. In a week. Or two.

It is the month when dress pants are suddenly too short and dress shoes are mysteriously too snug and schedules are too tight to do much about it. The time of year when you can't buy a white dress shirt for love or money.

In May, you are poor. The deposits are due for soccer camp and gymnastics camp and day camp and sleep-away camp and next year's school tuition. And the community pool has asked for your dues.

In May, you have to buy presents for the Sunday-school teachers and the grade-school teachers and the sitter who is graduating. You buy lovely annuals that will shrivel and burn by July, and you buy the truckloads of mulch that never seems to save them.

In May, the swim team manager schedules Wednesday for swimmers to try on this year's suit. (A new, more expensive style than the one you rinsed out all last summer so it would last two seasons.) But you can't make it, because Wednesday is also the day your daughter is scheduled to be photographed in her ballet recital costume. (You'll need an 8-by-11 for each set of grandparents.)

It is the month when you wash out uniforms every night like pantyhose, because rainy April has bunched up the sports schedule. In May, your leading hitter also plays lacrosse and your spot in the playoffs is in doubt. Not that you care. God, when will the season be over?

In May, you take the camcorder to the school strings concert and you notice that your son's bow is never going up when all the other bows are going up.

Your daughter has been asked to dance in the concert and you should be delighted, except that she plays the viola, too. You suspect she is dancing because she says she gets lost on the music page and so just plays whatever note she wants.

Everyone graduates from something in May or has a recital or their first holy communion or a confirmation or a bar mitzvah. And you have to throw a picnic or you have to go to one or you have to let your child go to one and worry if there will be drinking there.

May is the month of prom gowns that look like nightgowns and flowers and limos and boys you don't much like or boys who break girls' hearts.

May is the last chance you will have to read a book or clean house or have lunch with a friend or go to the grocery store by yourself, because soon the kids will be out of school and whining at you that they are bored and have nothing to do.

In May, your allergies bother you and your legs are so pale they reflect the sun. May is the month you try on bathing suits and remember that you are not young or thin.

In May, the kids' new shorts are always grass-stained the first day.

In May, you observe at your child's new school, and you meet with the new teachers and fill out the forms. But you don't realize your child is growing up until you see his long legs hanging out of the shorts that fit last summer.

In May, kids leave for school dressed too warmly and come home damp with sweat and smelling like puppies. In May, children don't want to do homework after dinner. They want to ride bikes or color with sidewalk chalk or play basketball. They are energized by the lengthening daylight, and you can't get them settled in bed.

In May, kids start to need baths again. In May, they want buzz haircuts.

In May, lunch boxes are in tatters. Backpacks come home loaded with the stuffings of lockers and desks.

In May, you clean the grill and eat outside because there are no bugs yet. The days are always warmer than you expect, the nights are always cooler.

In May, the grass is the color of jade, and you could cut it three times a week and you notice the wind again because you can hear it in the leaves of the trees.

In May, summer stretches out in front of you like a prairie.

# Taking it to the hoop

I GOT A basketball hoop for Mother's Day.

I know. I couldn't believe it myself. But there it is, a huge, free-standing basketball hoop, craning its neck over the driveway like a mechanical dinosaur.

How did I happen to get a basketball hoop for Mother's Day when a corsage would have done nicely?

Well, my husband went shopping with the children for my Mother's Day present. They went to a sporting goods store to buy the weightlifting gloves I'd hinted around for, found this basketball hoop instead and everyone got really wound up.

(That's right. Weightlifting gloves, not gardening gloves. But that is the stuff of another column.)

Anyway, the kids were so excited about the possibility of getting a basketball hoop that my husband had to take them home and give them a hot bath before they would settle down to sleep.

He had told them they had to clear it with me first, and, in any case, I had the station wagon and you just don't throw a 10-foot basketball hoop into the back seat of a car, no matter how many parts it comes in.

Outvoted as I was, I went to pick up the basketball hoop the next day while the children were in school, and they loved me for about 10 minutes when they arrived home and saw it in the back of the station wagon. When I told them I couldn't get it out of the car, let alone put it together, they stopped loving me.

(My husband responded to my report that the basketball hoop had been acquired by saying: "I don't know, honey. This is one of those purchases I would have thought twice about and then not done." "Thanks," I said.)

These things always take longer than you think, and so it was almost midnight when my husband had the hoop put together. The sun was not up the next morning, but my son was, waking the neighbors by clanging the ball off the rim.

Soon, there were children in my driveway whom I had never seen before, having what is known in the NBA as a "shoot-around," and my daughter had posted rules: "Take turns. No slam dunks. No fighting. See mom and dad for consequences."

By noon, all the juice in my fridge had been drunk, and all the snacks I had purchased for lunches the next week had been eaten. And all the flowers that line my driveway had been beaten to death.

Imagine an NBA game in which Charles Barkley repeatedly dives into the seats to retrieve loose balls. Imagine that, by halftime, every fan in the first six rows has been crushed or broken, and you have a pretty good idea of what my carefully tended flower beds looked like.

No one was more surprised than my husband when I did not go nuts. "That's OK," I said. "I want the kids here."

Now, let me say that hell is other people's children, and if I had wanted more than two kids, I would have had more than two kids. There are plenty of days when two is too many for me.

But I believe my sister was right when she used her winnings from a raffle to buy an air-hockey table and a used pinball machine instead of jewelry.

She added those toys to the TV, VCR and Super Nintendo that were already crowding her newly finished basement. Then she bought a used mini-fridge and filled it with soda and put her kitchen table and chairs down there, too.

The only place the poor woman can relax now is leaning against her kitchen counter with a cup of tea, but her basement looks like a youth center.

"That's OK," my sister said. "I want the kids here."

From Ellen, I learned that children in middle school and high school are in constant danger of flying out of the orbit that has kept them close to us. She has worked hard to draw her children and their friends back in, with a welcoming atmosphere, food, drink and amusements.

It has cost her in money and space and quietude, but she is reaping peace of mind. She knows where her children are, whom they are hanging with, and her gentle eavesdropping lets her hear what they are thinking.

From Ellen, I have learned that I should not mind the basketball hoop, the broken plants, the empty drink cups and the vanishing snacks. From Ellen, I have learned that I should not daydream about new furniture for my basement family room, but instead search the want ads for a used air-hockey table.

Maybe I can pick one up in time for Father's Day.

# Too beautiful for words

I BELIEVE A baby is born knowing all she will ever know, all that can be known.

I believe she has seen the face of God, that she comprehends the universe and can number the stars that sparkle above her cradle.

But soon enough, babies begin to talk. And when they try to fit all they know into an inadequate language, most of this knowledge falls away, lost forever. Soon their great wisdom shrinks to fit "ball" and "baby."

Claire Catherine Renaux died Tuesday of leukemia, three months short of her second birthday and, more importantly, without ever getting around to talking away all that she knew.

Claire's father is French, her mother is American. As is often the case with bilingual children, Claire understood every word said to her in French and English, but hadn't gotten around to speaking either language yet.

She managed to make her mind known with a vocabulary of finger-pointing as delicate as a princess might use to choose the fairy cakes for her afternoon tea, but as easy to understand as a first-grade primer.

And Claire enchanted me and all who met her. Without ever lifting one of those fingers, without ever saying a word.

The first meeting of Claire's parents, Kathy Helzlsouer and Jean-Luc Renaux, could have been a scene from a Cary Grant-Ingrid Bergman movie: the dining car of Il Palatino, the train linking Rome to Paris, in May 1990.

Kathy, a doctor and an associate professor at the Johns Hopkins School of Hygiene and Public Health, had just finished working in London and was doing some sightseeing before she returned to the United States. Jean-Luc, a manager in strategic marketing and international relations with the French railway system, SNCF, was returning from a meeting with Italian railroad officials. They were traveling in the same sleeping car and found themselves across the table from each other in the dining car one night.

"I wasn't sure, but there was something about him that made me want to know more," says Kathy. But there was no time, and she returned to Baltimore.

Two letters passed each other over the Atlantic and each said the same thing: This is crazy, but maybe it could work. Would you like to try? A trans-Atlantic courtship resulted in a wedding Aug. 3, 1991, in St. Vincent de Paul Church in Baltimore. Children were the first order of business. But when you are in your late 30s, that is easier wished for than accomplished, and Claire Catherine Renaux was hard won.

"It was harder than I ever thought it would be to get pregnant," says Kathy. "But I loved every minute of carrying her. I loved the morning sickness. I loved how hard she kicked. I loved how I felt every day.

"My friends wondered how I could have worked so hard to just give up my freedom, but I never minded. I loved holding her, rocking her. I never minded when she would get sick and keep us up at night. I loved it all.

"And I was never away from her."

Claire had a passport at 5 months of age and traveled everywhere with her parents.

When she was 6 months old, she went with them to Brussels, Belgium, stayed in the courtly Astoria Hotel, and was invited to dinner by one of Europe's top transportation executives.

Claire, dressed like a princess in mint-green velvet, began her life of conquests that night.

"She charmed everyone," says Jean-Luc. "The manager arrived and took pictures. She was delightful."

And Claire was with Kathy last May in Philadelphia when her mother presented a paper at a medical conference. But she was feverish, so Kathy and Jean-Luc returned to Baltimore, and Kathy missed the afternoon session.

The topic was acute myeloid leukemia, the deadliest form of leukemia.

Claire's fever passed, and her first birthday party went off as scheduled. "She perked up, but something was not right," says Kathy.

Claire was just learning to walk, so the bruises on her legs were no surprise. But the bruise on her ear troubled Kathy. She put it on her list of questions for Claire's well-baby checkup later that week.

Blood tests at that checkup alarmed Claire's pediatrician, Dr. Frances Gmur. It could be viral or it could be leukemia, she said.

Kathy looked at the slides. "My heart sank."

She knew what she was seeing. Kathy is not just a doctor. She is an oncologist. A cancer doctor.

Jean-Luc, working at home, grew alarmed when his wife and daughter did not return promptly. When Kathy called, he said, he realized within seconds that his daughter was likely to die.

"It was the most terrifying 25 minutes of my life," he says of that phone conversation. "I felt that I could not stand up."

On May 29, a bone marrow test confirmed the worst. Claire had AML. The bad leukemia.

There began the battle that Claire and Kathy and Jean-Luc would lose. From that day on, there was never any good news. Test results came back bad and worse. There were six courses of chemotherapy. Then a bone marrow transplant. Then more chemo. This was not just bad leukemia, this was smart leukemia.

"It was relentless," says Kathy. "No matter what we did, it found a way to outsmart us."

I am Claire's aunt by virtue of marriage and geography.

My sister and her husband are Claire's true aunt and uncle. But they live in another city, so when she was diagnosed with leukemia, I went to see her at the Johns Hopkins Children's Center on their behalf, having never laid eyes on the child myself and unsure even if I would recognize her mother from a casual meeting years before.

Claire was asleep that day, resting from the first of the chemotherapy, but I saw immediately why she was known in the family as "the most beautiful baby in the world." After an awkward reacquaintance with Claire's mother — my awkwardness, not hers — I went to the hospital parking lot and sobbed against the steering wheel of my car.

From that moment I was Claire's aunt. In the weeks and months of her hospitalization, I would visit as often as I could, hoping to find Claire awake and in the mood to play. I think she liked me. And I think it was because I was so much sillier than she and willing to repeat 100,000 times any game that made her laugh. She would wrinkle her nose, show all her teeth and give a little puff of a snort. Claire looked like Little Miss Mischief when she laughed.

I was bewitched by Claire, instantly, helplessly. When I finally came up for air, I realized that Kathy and Jean-Luc had allowed this to happen. They had gracefully and graciously let those of us who sought to succor them be comforted by Claire. They made every visitor to their hospital room feel needed and welcome until they were surrounded by a widening circle of broken hearts.

"There are two ways to face something like this," says Jean-Luc. "One is to be bitter to everyone who comes near you. The other is to face it, fight it and make sure she has a good time.

"We know we can die on any day. But we wanted to give Claire the best face and the best time that we could. That was our responsibility to her."

Visitors were startled when they found the proud parents smiling and photographing their daughter as she walked regally down the hospital hall, dressed up like a birthday cake and smiling and waving like she was the queen of the Rose Parade. At her side was the IV pole that pumped chemotherapy through a Hickman catheter into her chest.

"But this is part of her life," Jean-Luc would say as he snapped pictures.

When the sun set on the hospital day, when the visitors were gone, leaving behind offerings of food, Kathy and Jean-Luc would set the hospital tray table in front of the window, pull up two chairs and face each other over dinner. And they would pretend they were again on that train to Paris, falling in love as the Italian countryside rolled past.

Claire breezed through the worst of the treatments, always pleasant and as tough and resilient as the leukemia cells the treatments couldn't kill.

But nothing was ever hidden from Kathy, mother and cancer doctor. There was never a moment of blissful ignorance. "I wasn't able to have as much optimism as another mother might have," she says. "When people would tell me, 'It will be all right,' I could hope that was the case, but still, I knew the numbers."

While Claire napped, Kathy would slip across the street to her office in the Department of Epidemiology and search the world of medicine with her computer to find anything that might help Claire. Armed with all she knew as a doctor and all she was as a mother, Kathy was a formidable member of Claire's treatment team.

And yet all her knowledge did not help Claire.

"How much of a benefit was I to Claire? How can I say? The outcome was the same.

"But I could watch out for her."

Kathy never let the dreadful things she knew as a doctor intrude on the happy times she planned as Claire's mother.

On the day in July when they learned the worst news — that there was no remission — the family packed a picnic and went to Catoctin State Park. That evening the three went to dinner at a friend's home and the next day, Claire bounced to the beat of zydeco music at Artscape.

For Halloween, Kathy designed a costume around the beak-shaped sterile mask Claire had to wear and her niece, Jeannie Smith, sewed it for her. Claire was a duck. A feathery, yellow duck with orange tights on her legs and little webbed feet tied to the tops of her tennis shoes.

On their rare days of freedom from the hospital, there were trips to the zoo to see the "real" Babar or to the beach to see the ocean, to the airport to see the airplanes. Or they would walk to Patterson Park to swing and see the squirrels.

In this way, Jean-Luc and Kathy lived in the moment with Claire and they helped those who loved Claire do the same. Every day was complete in and of itself. If Claire was having a good day, we all had a good day. We would ask Jean-Luc, "How are you?" He would say, "Claire is alive today," and that was answer enough.

Claire drew all of us to her, spoke to us with her fingers, focused on us with her wise eyes, staying in the moment with us far longer than anyone had a right to expect. We stopped time and played because that was what she wanted from us.

During her last days, my visits became more frequent, but Claire could no longer acknowledge her Aunt Susan. Her last "words" to me looked like this: She raised her open hand and then curled her fingers down into her palm.

It was Claire's hand signal for "goodbye."

I believe Claire was born knowing all that she would ever know, all that can be known. I believe she comprehended the universe and could number the stars.

And I believe Claire was born knowing the heart against which she had rested, the dreams of the mother who carried her, nursed her and who cradled her as she slept away.

I believe Claire knew, too, why God did not answer the prayers that went up to him from around the globe to cure her, to save her. But, as articulate as she was with her delicate index finger, she would need words, lots and lots of words, to explain it to us.

Our comfort is this: We will live out our lives enchanted by Claire, her spell never broken. And, as it was with Claire, words will fail us forever.

# Chapter 6

# Vanities, *Confessions* & Secrets

# Let's pause for this message

I AM A WOMAN of a certain age.

I will not be more specific except to say that menopause is not a vocabulary word on my SATs but an event in my no longer distant future. And I will allow that I am closer to the end of my reproductive life than I am to the beginning of it.

I am trying to be upbeat about the approach of this watershed experience for women. I am trying to think of it as a spiritual transformation instead of another step toward the grave. I am trying to imagine myself as a re-energized and creative force rather than as a dried-up, empty husk.

And I was doing pretty well until I realized that, to an army of merchandisers and market analysts, I will soon be a dried-up, empty target audience.

I, and 40 million to 50 million of my girlfriends, will go through menopause sometime during the next decade. And, while 40 million to 50 million husbands may be dreading this, 40 million to 50 million sales reps are as excited about it as teen-age boys in heat.

They say a good advertising copywriter can sell ice to Eskimos, but they have met their match if they think they can sell menopause to those of us still carrying around mental pictures of ourselves as San Francisco flower children.

The first women of the baby boom generation will be 51 this year, the average age for the onset of menopause. While feminists and New Agers try to convince us that we will ride an unimagined energy burst into a new creative season, most of us believe we will leave our 51st birthday party and break a hip getting into the car.

Falling levels of estrogen, the hormone produced by the ovaries, affects the normal functioning of many body systems, including skin, bone, blood vessels and sex organs. A catalog of health problems arise from, or are complicated by, menopause: hot flashes, night sweats, fatigue, vaginal dryness, frequent urination, sour taste, body odor and painful indigestion.

And, of course, dreaded mood swings.

I tried to give my husband a heads-up on this life transition, and all he could think to ask was, "Is it worse than now?"

"It is like now," I replied, "only all the time." He crossed himself and returned to his newspaper.

I don't know why I even brought it up, except that it is all anyone seems to be talking about these days.

When they start lacing orange juice with calcium and promoting it as a supplement for menopausal women, you know you have a bull's eye pinned to your back.

When Johnson & Johnson starts calling its old K-Y jelly the answer to "feminine dryness," you know they don't think you are changing diapers any longer. (My guess is, the euphemism departments of ad agencies are working a lot of late nights.)

The generation of women who wanted infinite detail about every minute of child-bearing has hit a vacuum on the complex subject of menopause because doctors are too busy shuttling them in and out of their paper gowns in a managed-care rush to answer their questions.

Leave it to marketing experts to move into that vacuum. They are the ambulance chasers of the advertising industry, but they have learned some lessons. They no longer are pitching products with slogans such as "Menrium treats the menopausal symptoms that bother him the most." But they still are trying to make a buck off women.

There are hormones and hormone patches, vitamins and herbs, hygiene products, cooling blankets, soy breads and hormone-laced face creams, special clothes and exercise products. When a trio of California businesswomen launched a mail-order catalog offering this variety of stuff, they couldn't believe their luck.

What's next, the Menopause Home Shopping Channel?

Somebody declared June to be Menopause Month. There is a hot-flash support group calling itself Red Hot Mamas. Some company named its vaginal lubricant "Moist Again."

And financial analysts are referring to incontinence as a "very attractive and overlooked market."

I don't think so.

Does anybody else find this ridiculous, intrusive and exploitative, or am I just in the middle of a mood swing?

I am sure my pre-menopausal rage will cause some man to write and say that 50-something women ought to be glad somebody is pursuing them for something, that somebody finds them attractive, even if it is only their purchasing power that excites.

All I can say in response is this: When the highways are dotted with billboards advertising products that target the great, untapped impotence market, we'll talk again.

# To sleep, perchance?

IT'S 5 P.M. It is the dinner hour, and you are looking down the barrel of I'm-starving, yuck-what-is-this-stuff-anyway, I-forgot-my-mathbook-at-school, he's-splashing-soap-in-my-eyes, read-me-a-story, getme-a-drink and can-you-snuggle-with-me. And you are facing it alone.

The remote control, the evening paper, the aroma therapy bath, your *Vanity Fair*. All are at least four hours away. On a good night.

The dinner-homework-bedtime routine is endless, but seems particularly so to a special brand of widows. Women whose husbands work late.

In the era of tag-team child care, where each spouse takes a different shift, women often find themselves alone and tense, and bedtime can seem a lifetime away. (Why don't I remember any intimate routines from my own childhood? Am I in denial here or did my mother just say, "Good night. Get to bed"?)

My husband does not get home until after the damage has been done. He arrives full of energy and chat and wondering if the kids are asleep yet. I tell him that if he is not part of the solution, he is part of the problem. And if he wakes them up and starts this whole drill over again, I will have the locks changed.

I am not very civil. But how can I be? I am a drill sergeant as I march my children inexorably toward bed.

Clear your dishes to the sink. Let me wipe the kitchen table first. I know you know how to spell those words, but humor me. All the signs on the paper are subtraction signs; you're not supposed to add. I can't read that, and your teacher will think I'm a bad mother if I let you turn it in looking like that. Let's not splash the water all over the floor. They don't look like they've been brushed to me. Just two stories, Mommy is tired. God bless Gramma, God bless Grampa. I will snuggle with you in a minute, Jessie is sad about something. Joe, if you needed to find a picture of fruit, you should have told me before now. Good night. Mommy's day is over.

My sister, Cynthia, has four children, so her days last twice as long as mine. Sometimes, she gets so desperate she starts the routine at 4 p.m.

because she thinks she can fool them into bed earlier. Do you know what it does to women like us when they turn the clocks ahead in the spring?

Homework has made Cynthia gray before her time. Her oldest has been claiming for nine years that he did it all at school. Her second child is the kind who remembers at 9 p.m. that he needs 24 Halloween cupcakes or a shepherd's costume for school the next day. Her daughter dissolves into tears if her homework has any eraser marks on it.

When her youngest started school and then acted baffled by some paper he was supposed to color at home, she just lost it, started shrieking: "I'm done with first grade. I have done it four times. I only needed to do it once."

But children are so needy at night. They are tired, and the homework seems impossible. Cooperation is beyond them. Their troubles overrun them. They are sad and angry, and the day's injustices come rushing back to them. And there will be no peace until you soothe them. Maybe your teacher was just having a bad day. Kids say mean things, just ignore them. Tomorrow will be a better day.

I have a romantic, idealized vision in my head of quiet, civilized evenings by the fire. The kids snuggled next to me as I read aloud from D'Aulaires' "Greek Myths." What do I get instead? Emotional meltdowns all around. I want to comfort them. I want them to go to bed with a happy heart. But mostly I want them to go to bed.

Suddenly, they are asleep. I am always amazed at how quickly they drop off. Like throwing a light switch. That fast. One minute, they are giving you their list of demands for breakfast, and the next minute, they are drooling lightly on their pillows.

I stand by the door and watch them sleep. Illuminated by the hall light, Jessie's tumbled red curls shine. Joe's fingers flex slightly in his sleep. Is he shifting the grip on his bat in some dreamland ball field? Their cheeks are slightly puffy and pink. Their foreheads are damp from the exertion of the day's last hours.

I want to wake them and tell them that I love them. That I'm sorry I was cross. That we will have a better day tomorrow. We'll build a fire after dinner, I whisper to them, and my hand on their cheeks does not wake them. I will read you a Greek myth.

# PMS: Positively Mental Syndrome?

IT WAS YEARS ago, when those of us who spoke of premenstrual syndrome were on the cutting edge of New Wave feminist topics, and I was trying to explain this curse to a male friend.

"We are not talking about water-retention and mild irritability here," I said.

"We are talking about volcanic rage sandwiched between bouts of helpless weeping and episodes of timidity so severe that driving a car takes more assertiveness than you can muster. And these feelings come and go with the cyclical precision of the tides.

"I have three sisters, and one can tell of mood swings wilder than the other. This is real, but it can't be normal."

He paused to consider. "Are you sure y'all aren't just bitches?" he asked.

Years later, the American Psychiatric Association has provided me with my snappy comeback. We're not bitches. We're mentally ill.

Great. Hey, what a relief. And all this time, I thought I was just an inadequate person, that I was suffering from an acute case of failure-to-cope.

Instead, I learn that I am not just the victim of poisonous hormone surges that flood the real me right out the door. I have a "depressive disorder."

The soon-to-be published edition of the APA's Diagnostic and Statistical Manual of Mental Disorders refers to severe forms of PMS as "premenstrual dysphoric disorder" or PMDD. It is described as "a pattern of severe, recurrent symptoms of depression and other negative mood states, that occurs in the last week of the menstrual cycle and markedly interferes with daily living." No kidding.

This definition, and the decision to classify it as a mental illness, was arrived at after five years of discussion by an APA study group. But even the members of the study group could not agree among themselves that PMDD should be so classified. They could not agree on the symptoms, the cause or the treatment.

And for a woman, coming to terms with PMDD is just as difficult.

Where does a woman start when the volume of her anger makes her ears ring? When she finds herself standing outside herself, watching someone she doesn't recognize, but is powerless to comfort or to calm? Is this a behavioral problem, a function of the kinds of pressures women are under, or is it chemically induced? Is there some receptor in the brain that, for some reason, becomes more or less responsive to the ebb and flow of estrogen during a woman's cycle? No one knows.

Women are loath to mention it, except in exchanges of black humor with friends. It sounds too much like the old alibi, "Don't mind me, I have my period." We stopped using that excuse when we stopped using Harriet Nelson and Donna Reed as role models.

The APA estimates that only 3 percent of women suffer from PMDD. What a coincidence. They all live near me.

A physician friend once mused that if she asked every woman on whom she performed routine gynecological examinations if she was experiencing anything that might fit the description of PMDD, "I bet I'd be blown away by the response."

There are more than 150 symptoms assigned to PMDD, and a woman can spend a lot of time flogging herself for failings in her character before she looks at her calendar and sees a pattern.

What happens when she mentions these vague — and face it, bitchy — symptoms to her doctor? The range of treatments only illustrates how little is known about this malady.

Avoid caffeine and alcohol. Take anti-depressants. Go on The Pill. Take vitamin B-6. Take magnesium. Eat pasta. Take estrogen or take progesterone. Don't skip meals, avoid junk food. Join a support group. Pamper yourself with naps and romance novels. See a therapist.

A British doctor and well-known author on health topics, Caroline Shreeve, advised women sufferers not to drive, ride a bicycle or attend important meetings during this time in their cycle. She also wrote that women should wear dark glasses, use worry beads and reserve a special outfit for PMS days. "Try to avoid black — it's far too funereal," is her advice.

Does it sound like we are guessing here? Why not add: Have a hysterectomy. Take a lover. Join Club Med. Try yoga. See an acupuncturist, see a hypnotist. Buy yourself something pretty.

Considering what we don't know about PMS, they all make about as much sense.

A depressive disorder? You bet women get depressed. You'd be depressed, too, if you felt like this and the only explanations you have are: You're a bitch or you're crazy.

# A slice of life

PIZZA WAS created more than 100 years ago by an Italian chef who combined the colors of the Italian flag (red, green and white) in a dish to please the king's consort.

No longer a royal delicacy, pizza is today as common as the penny, as easy to find and just about as cheap. And it is so American that we continue to believe we invented it.

The large, flat cardboard box has replaced the hearth and the television set as the icon around which the American family gathers. If we surveyed Americans, I'm sure we'd find that families are more likely to have a regular pizza night than to go to church on Sunday.

If not for pizza, the frustrated American mother, unwilling to scrape another supper into the sink, would send her children to bed hungry. The fact that there are no dishes to wash is a bonus for her.

Pizza is the hard currency of our relationship with these children. We can trade the promise of a Domino's pizza for their cooperation in everything from housework to homework. (They are more cheered by the sight of the delivery guy's car than they are by their father returning from a business trip.)

Pizza is how we get out of mealtime jams created by their busy lives. Pizza is how we make a shopping trip special when the purchases will not be for them.

Pizza lubricates the social life of adults, too. We can always get together by agreeing to order pizza for the kids; our children will go anywhere as long as we tell them there will be pizza for the kids. You can serve your guests any fancy meal you want because you can always order pizza for the kids. Having a children's birthday party? Order pizza for the kids.

Pizza is our excuse to get together as a family. We think we are having quality time with our children; they think we are eating pizza. Even teens will agree to be seen with their parents in public if the family is going out for pizza. Dinner out with the family isn't ruinously expensive, because you are only having pizza. And you can usually get a beer in a pizza joint.

You can teach your children to cook using pizza. The first "meal" they make in a middle-school home economics class is the classic pizza bagel. This skill, more than staying home without a sitter, makes them feel all grown-up and independent.

Pizza is the one food that is not particularly good out of the microwave, so a child must learn to preheat an oven and to find the middle oven rack to cook a pizza. Doctoring your own pizza with a little more cheese, oregano and pepperoni is the height of gourmet cookery. I don't know if much more in the way of kitchen skill is needed these days.

I could pave my yard and carpet my house in the pizza my family has eaten during the last year alone. Really. *Pizza Today* magazine says Americans consume more than 100 acres of pizza every day, or 350 slices per second. Now that is fast food.

Frozen pizza is the hottest item in the grocery store — sales are up 40 percent in the last six years, according to a definitive history of pizza in *Smithsonian* magazine. But it had better be Tombstone and not one of those shrink-wrapped numbers from the deli department. My children wouldn't eat one of those if they were starving.

Pizza also serves as a universal and very elastic unit of measure. The whining response: "I just had a slice of pizza," can be interpreted to mean "I'm not hungry for whatever it is you are thinking about serving" or "I'm starving. How long does it take to get a meal around here, anyway?" When spoken by an adult, "I just had a slice of pizza" means "I didn't break my diet, I just bent it a bit."

My fellow mothers and I frown and complain that all our children ever want to eat is pizza, but we are not being fair, because if we are honest, that's all we ever want to serve them. And if we believe that tomato sauce is a vegetable, we can do it without remorse. When you serve pizza, you can be sure their bellies are full, and that, along with an occasional multivitamin, will make you feel that you are a good mother.

After all, if that Italian chef a century ago had been asked to create a diet staple for the American family instead of a treat for a queen, he could not have done better than pizza.

# Glamour, shmamour

"I WILL NEVER look this good again."

Once you are on this side of 40 and the decline begins, you can say that to yourself every morning with some certainty. You will never again look as good as you do right now.

But this is particularly and painfully true as I look at the photographs made of me at Elegant Images in Columbia Mall. Hair poofed to the max. Makeup as thick as peanut butter. Bare shoulders skimmed by satin and silk. I will never look this good again.

I went — in the name of investigative journalism — in a work shirt, khaki shorts and my yuppie mommy white Keds. No makeup and no curling iron. I wanted the transformation to be complete. And it was. I had no idea I was so beautiful.

Glamour isn't my style. I am a workaholic mom whose clothes and makeup have all the zip of 'Nilla Wafers. I once prepared for a fancy Christmas party by having my nails manicured red, and my daughter thought she'd finally gotten the Sparkle Beach Barbie mom she thought she deserved.

My husband says he likes me "plain," and I never have had the nerve to ask if that means he likes me without adornment or if he likes me because I am plain. His response to my trips to the hairdresser is: "What's wrong, honey? When you have problems, they usually come out in your hair."

But the folks at Elegant Images understand me. As I sit in the make-up chair and watch April Jurasevich's sponges and brushes uncover the me that was there all along, she predicts that I will say what everyone says when they see the finished product: "That doesn't even look like me." And she is right.

There are plenty of women who want not to look like themselves for at least one afternoon. Elegant Images, a franchise and subsidiary of Segall-Majestic Inc., the Baltimore company that has been doing my children's school photos for years, is booked solid most weekends.

I spend three hours in a cross between a beauty salon and a model's photography session. After Kelly Loudermilk goes after my droopy locks with a rat-tail comb and a can of hair spray, there is a wall of dress-up clothes for me to choose from: furs, denims, leathers, lace, jewels and sequins.

Some trick lighting and some soft focus camera work, and I look like Joan Collins, Heather Locklear or Cher. Benefit Ball Barbie or Biker Barbie. Take your pick. And all for not much more than the cost of those family portraits we do every couple of years.

"Before Christmas and Valentine's Day are our busiest times," says owner Billie Roogow. "Wives, girlfriends. Women want to do this as a gift to their husbands or boyfriends."

And maybe to themselves.

"Everyone can be more glamorous than they are," says Billie diplomatically when I ask what kinds of miracles her staff has had to perform.

I feel awkward in my costumes and the gaudy jewelry, but the photographer melts my reserve with his boisterous cheerleading: "God, you're great! What a smile! Give me another one. Are you sure you don't do this for a living? You look incandescent."

And I feel incandescent. As if I am glowing from someplace inside. Where have these black lace gloves been all my life? How could I not have known how spectacular I look in a beaded bodice?

It is over too quickly, and I am back in my khakis and my Keds, padding toward my car, looking from the neck up like Sharon Stone. Feeling kind of silly, looking as good as I do in a mall full of half-nuts bare-faced mothers doing their Saturday errands.

When they see me, my family recoils. They try to be polite — I think they know I will cry — but even my daughter takes a step back. "I think they did too much, Mom," she says.

Hurt and trying not to show it, I leave to drive around the neighborhood, hoping to find a girlfriend to giggle with. Someone needs to see how beautiful I am before I no longer am.

There must be witnesses.

Back home, I pucker my lips in the mirror before I step into the shower. They make a luscious rose and satin bow. I didn't know my mouth was so pretty.

The water washes the temporarily new me down the drain. The me I knew I was all along. The me I will never be again.

And I think to myself that I will start to wear lipstick.

# Tailbone's connected to the . . . friends

THE BEST THING about aerobics is knowing that in a little more than an hour it will be over and I will be able to have a doughnut and take a nap.

I also like aerobics because it is an escape from all the troubles that buzz in my head. You can't think during aerobics or you will fall down.

Well, I must have been thinking the other day in aerobics, because I fell down.

That miserable excuse for a joint at the bottom of my leg, that made-in-Taiwan ankle of mine, gave way as I placed my foot on the aerobic step. I had this sensation of stepping off into thin air.

And I fell.

Fell right on my, well, "po-po," as Miss Sandy says in my daughter's ballet class. (As in: "Ladies, let's tuck in our po-pos.")

I landed full force on my tailbone and cracked it. I remember thinking as I hit the floor and slipped into that black pool of pain, "Well, Susan, you're not walking away from this one."

And I didn't. They carried me to the lobby of the health club, laid me on my tummy, put an ice pack on my po-po, took an accident report and left me there.

I faded in and out of pain, and knew I was not going to make it home. As the hard bodies gathered for the next class (Super Step, during which you dance like Shirley Temple on a staircase), I asked one of them to call my husband. The Super Steppers, in their Jogbras and their thong leotards and their Lycra shorts, were gathered around me when he arrived.

"You guys better split," I said, my voice thick with pain. "If he sees all of you in those get-ups, he will break out in hives."

(My husband buys me the latest aerobic outfits for birthdays. But when I put them on for class, he says: "You're not going to leave the house in that, are you?")

When I saw Gary, I burst into tears. I could not get up. I could not walk. I was not the capable woman he had married.

"I'm calling an ambulance," he said.

"You will not," I said, recovering quickly. "I will not leave here like that. Not in front of all these women. Do you understand me?" My teeth were clenched in pain and determination.

So instead, my husband backed the station wagon up to the health club door, opened the tailgate, put the back seat down and loaded me in like a piece of plywood. He did everything but leave the hatch open and tie a red flag to my toe. It occurred to me that an ambulance might have been more dignified.

Gary off-loaded me to the couch, gave me an ice bag and left for work. That is how my children found me after school.

"Oh, great," said my devoted son, flinging his backpack in frustration. "I suppose this means I can't have friends over today."

He didn't even bother to ask if I was going to walk again.

My daughter (who, I am now certain, will be the one who visits me in the nursing home after my son puts me there) gently patted my head. "I like your aerobics outfit, Mom," she said. "Is it new?"

There I lay for three days, in a fog of pain and pain-killers. (Drugs, I am convinced, don't kill pain. You still hurt, you just don't care.) I watched helplessly as my children made their own snacks, watched what they wanted on TV, dragged out every toy they own, did not pick up after themselves and ignored me.

My son came to me that first night as I drifted into a chemically induced sleep on the sofa. "Mom, I don't want to pressure you or anything. But, like, how soon till I can have friends over?"

During the days of my confinement, my husband made brief appearances and said, "You poor thing."

But, like soldiers when one of their own has fallen, my women friends rescued me. Meals and flowers arrived. Prescriptions and groceries were delivered. One friend even brought worms for the frogs.

Any incapacity to a mother — from the flu to a dread disease — is a disaster the scope of which only other women can understand. It takes eight people to do the job of any one of us.

So, women from all over the neighborhood swept my children away, delivered them to soccer and ballet, made them do their homework and fed them.

One of them said to my son, "You know what's next, don't you, Joe?"

"Yeah," he said, his voice world-weary. "There's a column in this somewhere. But it's her butt she broke. At least she won't be quoting me again."

# To-do list

DO YOU KNOW anyone who flosses? Actually flosses. Not people who say they floss. They could be lying. Not someone who talks about how important flossing is. She could just be a dental hygienist. But someone whom you have actually seen flossing.

Of course not. And not just because you don't hang around in bathrooms. You don't know anyone who flosses because no one does, despite how important flossing is. No one flosses because, like you, they don't have time.

They don't have time to be the kind of person who flosses. Or the kind of person who rubs cuticle cream on her fingertips each night.

Like you, I have read all those helpful hints in magazines while waiting in the dentist's office to see the dental hygienist and get a lecture on flossing. I know what I should be doing to be a better person, a better parent, a better homeowner, a kinder spouse, a considerate friend, a more productive worker.

They are all worthy tasks. I just don't have time to do them.

And yet I am morbidly drawn to these admonitions in magazines and on "Regis and Kathie Lee." I listen earnestly to the suggestions of everyone from my plumber to my manicurist. The result is, I am walking around with these lists in my head of all the things I am not doing. And I am feeling bad about it.

But every day is a new day, and, just as I promise myself each morning that I will only have a light snack for supper, I vow to make time to do all these things I know I should be doing.

Such as . . .

Drink 64 ounces of water each day to moisturize my skin from the inside out. Chew each bite of food 30 times while not reading the newspaper or watching television, so that my stomach can send my brain the message that I am full.

Stretch before I exercise and again after I exercise. Exercise.

Divide my perennials in early March. Spend a few minutes in prayer or meditation each morning and each evening. Start saving for college now.

Read 100 pages of a book every night before bed. Polish my copper. Plan dinner menus for a week, make a shopping list from the menus and buy only those items at the grocery store — which I visit only on a full stomach.

Run vinegar through the coffee maker, keep a journal, sprinkle baking soda on the carpets before I vacuum. Cook with fresh herbs. Focus on just five areas of conflict with my child and resolve those.

Wash my makeup off before bed, sort my paperbacks and give them to the library, touch my mate in a loving but non-sexual way at least once a day.

Give away any clothes that I have not worn in two years. Check my children one last time before bed to make sure they are covered.

Learn a new word, bake with my children, rent the video of a movie that won an Academy Award.

Eat five fruits a day, read at least one item on the editorial page of my newspaper and find someone to discuss it with. Watch a video of an old musical with my children.

Treat that spot now so it will come out when I do laundry later.

Practice math facts with my children every night. Practice spelling words with my children every night. Read to my children every night. Say prayers with my children every night. Moisturize my face and hands every night.

Build bone mass and prevent osteoporosis by doing weight-bearing exercise. Turn off the water while I brush my teeth.

Listen for those signals that my children want to talk. Treat myself to a candlelight bath with aroma-therapy oils.

Celebrate each holiday by doing a craft with my kids. Make sure they call or write thank-you notes for gifts. Wash the outside of the windows, too.

Flip the mattresses on all the beds and wash all the bedclothes. Plan a date with my husband every week and a weekend getaway every month. Pinch off the bleeders on my tomato plants.

Spread crab grass preventer in early March. Post affirmations on the bathroom mirror where I will see them every morning. ("I am happily and easily living without a credit card.")

Cut up the credit cards.

Subscribe to the opera/symphony/ballet/theater. And go.

Eliminate meat, alcohol, caffeine, soda and cheese from my diet. Find a new recipe and make it.

Spend time alone with one child. Make an appointment with my gynecologist.

Floss.

# Forecast: scattered divorces

THERE IS DIVORCE in the air around me.

The conditions have been right for a while — the barometric pressure of our lives has been dropping — so we look into the sky, into the horizon for what we can feel coming. Divorce is in the air. You can smell it, like rain.

Not me. Not yet. If I'm lucky, if my kids are lucky, maybe never. But there are divorces all around me, among couples closer and closer to us, and I fear one will strike us. Like a virus. Somebody in your neighborhood comes down with it. Just wait. It will get to you.

I am not surprised by these divorces. Because this time in our lives — when our marriages and our kids are in their teens, when each year brings the need to disguise another body part, when it becomes clear that our lives will not turn out as we had planned — is the perfect time, the perfect incubation, for divorce. A petri dish of discontent. Divorce may be our last bold act, our last chance for true love or freedom or starting over.

So I am not surprised, just afraid. I feel vulnerable. Will it strike me, or him?

We are awash in the fatigue and chaos of two jobs, two cars, two kids, and our conversations sound something like: "Will you be home in time to pick up the kids?" We have no time to examine our marriage to determine its health. I don't think we have any movies in common anymore, but it has been so long I can't be certain. Is that the first sign that your marriage is over? When you can't agree on a movie?

How did these couples know they had to divorce? He didn't beat her, she didn't drink. He didn't gamble away the mortgage, she kept a nice house. No other man, no other woman. No obvious reason to divorce. Nothing you could see from the outside. Just a phone call after a long silence, when they start to tell their friends, "It's over."

"I can't bad-mouth him. I have the kids to think about. They still need to love him," she will say when you ask why.

But there is a reason. There always is. And after a while, it will leak out and we will all know why. But it might not be the real reason. It might be the distillation of a lot of reasons. It might just be their spin on it, his spin, her spin.

"I don't want you to have to pick sides in this," she will say. "You can be his friend."

His friend, her friend? I don't want to be anybody's friend. I don't want to get too close. It might be catching. If they can hate their life enough to turn it all upside down, knowing why might make me hate my life, too. Their marriage looked as good as mine feels. If it wasn't, mine might not be, either.

But there is a morbid curiosity, isn't there? I cannot imagine the pain and turmoil of splitting up a family, so I want to know what made them do it. What was so bad that the tears of the children could be better?

The children. "They will be better off. There will be no more fighting." Divorce starts here and then moves on to a benign notion of civilized co-parenting. Sometimes it works out that way. Sometimes the kids are not the weapon.

But it's naive to think that separate but equal parenting makes kids happy.

We have demanded that our husbands be more than breadwinners, that they be nurturers, too. And they have responded to an extent that makes divorce doubly horrific for the children. For years, the courts thought it cruel and unthinkable to separate a child from its mother. Now, it is equally cruel to separate them from their fathers.

Children are tangled up in love with their fathers in a way our generation was not. Our fathers were often remote or working late or simply undemonstrative, unaccustomed to intimacy with children.

Our children's fathers are not that way because we refused to allow it. My sister's husband was the one at home the first time their daughter shaved her legs. She ran naked from the bathtub in triumph at not having nicked herself, and he gathered her up in an unself-conscious hug. He will probably be the one at home when she starts her period, and that will not be a problem for any of them.

Remove that father and there will be more than an empty chair at dinner; there will be a hole in that child's life that can't be filled by weekend visits.

But these couples know that. They know all of this. And yet they are still divorcing. I can't imagine how much trouble, anger or pain there was in these marriages if divorce is better.

And that scares me more than the rest.

# Calendar girl

JUST IN TIME for your holiday shopping: the Susan Reimer Tearaway Calendar. Three hundred sixty-five days of Susan Reimer. A lively quote, a muttered curse, a sardonic comment or biting sarcasm for each day of the year. The perfect gift for the newspaper reader who really enjoyed Susan Reimer's last column, but can't remember what it was about.

Purchase a shopping bag full of these desktop calendar cubes for Christmas. They make ideal gifts for women friends, thoughtful neighbors and your children's teachers.

Each calendar comes in its own brightly colored box, so you won't need to sit cross-legged on the floor at 2 a.m. wrapping them in time for the children to forget to take them to the school party the next day.

I came up with this absolutely unoriginal money-making scheme after seeing calendar cubes displayed at all those kiosks that suddenly crowd the malls at holiday time and make shopping that much more difficult to navigate.

Everybody who is anybody — and some people who aren't anybody — markets his own tearaway calendar, and I want one, too.

Sports teams, beer, bad jokes, cartoon characters, television shows.

Even collective nouns, inanimate objects and offensive remarks have their own tearaway calendars.

I am a real person, even if no one I live with thinks of me that way, and I should be able to get someone to make me into a calendar.

Joshua doesn't even exist, and he has his own calendar — 365 days of the fictional Jesus figure from the novels by Joseph F. Girzone.

There is a duct tape calendar — 365 things you can do with it. There is a Beatles calendar — 365 days of a group that hasn't recorded together in 26 years.

The pope has a calendar. So does radio adviser Dr. Laura. The title of her calendar is "Now Go and Take the Day," but I think she stole it from the pope.

Dilbert, Ziggy, Mickey, Cathy, Pooh and Garfield have tearaway calendars that recycle single panels from the funny papers. I can do that: 365 of the best paragraphs I have written. That's perfect for me because

I have kids, and I haven't been able to write more than one sensible paragraph at a time in years.

I don't have to worry about who I am offending now that Jeff Foxworthy has crossed the threshold of taste with his "You Might Be a Redneck If ..." tearaway calendar. An example: "You might be a redneck if there is more carpet on your toilet than on your floors."

And I don't have to worry about the quality of my work because the "Random Acts of Kindness" calendar has collected a year's worth of thoughts not worth thinking, let alone remembering: "Greatness comes in all shapes and sizes and most true heroes are unsung."

Hey, I can write stuff like that. Easy.

There are calendars for cars, for gardeners, for cats, dogs and TV shows: "Friends," "Jeopardy!," "Star Trek." "Wheel of Fortune." The Nick at Nite calendar has this entry for Dec. 13: "Dick Van Dyke's birthday. A great day to trip over furniture."

Do people get paid a lot of money to do this? I need to know.

You can change your life with one of these calendars, and I want to change mine. "Simplify Your Life." "I Can Do It." "Stop the Insanity." "The 7 Habits of Highly Effective People," which covers only the first week in January. "The Road Less Traveled." "Men are From Mars, Women are From Venus." "Meditations for Women Who Do Too Much."

How about one titled: "The Pay Off Susan Reimer's Home Equity Loan" calendar?

Beavis and Butthead have a calendar. So does John Bradshaw. The "Healing the Shame that Binds You" calendar. What were they thinking when they titled that bad boy?

I was going to buy the Cosmopolitan "Nice Girl's Guide to Sensational Sex" calendar for each of my women friends. "Daily tips for red-hot lovemaking," read the label. But it occurred to me none of us would live long enough to use 365 sex tips.

There is a calendar for everyone on your shopping list — even middle-school boys who go through life not remembering what day it is: "Snaps. The funniest, rudest and most creative snaps, caps and insults." Example: "If ugliness were bricks, your mother would be a housing project."

I am working hard to make sure my tearaway desk-top calendar is at your mall kiosk in time for the holidays.

Next year, I am hoping to mass-market the "Susan Reimer Exercise Video," featuring me carrying 12 bags of groceries from the car while my lazy children pretend not to hear me calling them.

I have plans, too, for the "Susan Reimer Beauty Book," with helpful advice such as "Don't apply mascara when the car is accelerating," and "Don't let your husband see you putting on pantyhose."

And this is just the beginning.

Ideas? You bet. I have 365 of them.

# You snooze, you lose

THE LAST THING I remember is pulling the afghan across my legs and listening to the sounds of my children playing basketball outside. The afternoon sun glinted through my open bedroom window and fell across my face, warm and bright.

And then I napped.

Downstairs, my husband had simply lost consciousness while reading the newspaper on the couch. It was Saturday afternoon, and a morning of soccer games had made us feel as though we'd put in a full day's work.

He had simply passed out. That is how men nap, I think. Accidentally. But my nap had been deliberate. Anticipated.

I had made no pretense of reading. I curled up in the pile of throw pillows on my bed and shut my eyes as the overly warm fall breezes puffed the curtains and made the last of the leaves rustle outside my window.

I had one purpose: to sleep in the middle of the day.

Napping is a guilty pleasure in this country. We are too pressed by our list of things to do to give into a nap. And too ashamed to admit it if we do.

Falling asleep in front of the television is acceptable, but most of us have not intentionally napped since our babies gave up naps in time to start school.

"I used to take them when the kids took them," said my sister Cynthia. She has four kids and those naps were the only reason she didn't go crazy.

"Even when they were in kindergarten, I used to put them down for a nap when they came home from school. They were taking naps when they weren't tired because I needed one."

Now, she can't relax enough to sleep during the day. There is too much pressure to get something done. But she daydreams about them: "Right after lunch. A few pages of a romance novel and then an afghan pulled up to my chin.

"But I don't even stop to have lunch anymore."

Scientists at the National Sleep Foundation tell us that a nap has less to do with how many kids you have or how much sleep you didn't get the night before than it does with your biological rhythms.

Between 3 a.m. and 5 a.m., the human body is overcome with the need to sleep. Twelve hours later — between 3 and 5 in the afternoon — that urge returns. A heavy lunch or a boring meeting only heightens the feeling.

This afternoon seems to suggest that the human body was meant to nap. A quarter of an hour is usually enough to improve concentration and performance.

My friend Nan told me about a doctor who would take an afternoon nap in his office with his keys in his hand and his arm stretched over a tin pie pan.

When his hand relaxed enough to release the keys into the pan, the clatter woke him for the next patient. That taste of sleep was all he needed.

A nap of more than a half-hour, the National Sleep Foundation says, and our circulation slips into the sleep mode. We wake groggy and sluggish and it takes longer to get going again, although the benefits of that sleep will last for hours: improved alertness, sharper memory and generally reduced symptoms of fatigue.

Naps are not a substitute for a good night's sleep. But, the NSF says, an occasional restorative nap — so-called power naps — can help us tap into the "alertness reserve" the doctor apparently found.

If this is true, why do we continue to regard naps as a waste of time or evidence of sloth?

Why do we say things like "steal a nap" or "catch a nap"? Why sleep in the car while waiting to pick up the kids or in front of the television, when there are afghans and throw pillows waiting upstairs? Why push ourselves through our weekends the way we push ourselves through the workday?

In his book, "The Art of Napping," Boston University professor and sleep researcher William Anthony says we live in a "napist" society, full of people who make others ashamed of napping or who hide their own naps.

"We should consider it in tandem with productivity, not in opposition to it," Anthony said in an interview with CNN.

My nap that Saturday afternoon was the first in many years, but I didn't do it to increase my productivity or my mental acuity. My nap was an end in itself. It was my purpose to nap for the pure pleasure of it. That nap was about as goal-oriented as eating a piece of chocolate cake would be.

Maybe that is the reason we deny ourselves the delicious luxury of sleeping in the middle of the day.

"It would be cool and rainy," my friend Nan says, spinning out her nap fantasy. "And the windows would be open just a bit and I would pull a comforter up to my chin. I would lie on my back, princess style, as my mother used to call it, and relax all my muscles.

"It would not be a cat nap. I am a world-class sleeper and if I am going to nap, I am going to nap."

# Emotional hangovers

I WOKE FEELING as though my head were stuffed with cotton and my mouth were lined with it.

It had been a tough night, full of restlessness and illustrated by those dreams that come to you when you are more awake than asleep. Vivid, anxious dreams that are more like unrestrained worry than dreams. Dreams that stay with you, like the taste of garlic.

For the rest of the day, I rocked between agitation and exhaustion. In my head, I sorted through every word I had said the night before, replayed every scene. Wishing it had not happened, wishing I could erase the loop of videotape in my brain.

At work, my thinking was thick and slow, clotted with remorse. My shame left me weary and wanting the forgetfulness of sleep.

The symptoms were familiar. I had another hangover. But not the kind you get from too much wine. It was the kind of hangover you get from too much anger.

It was an emotional hangover.

I don't know if men have emotional hangovers, but women do.

It is regret with physical symptoms. It is where the expression "sick at heart" comes from. An emotional hangover is what you feel when you can't let go of your bad behavior. Not because you embarrassed yourself, although you certainly did that, but because you behaved badly toward the people you love, the people whose care you have been given.

My son had forgotten to lock the house when he left for soccer practice and my husband had forgotten to lock the house when he came to bed and I exploded in rage all out of proportion to the crimes they had committed.

Even in the midst of my fury, I knew it was not about deadbolts, but about something else entirely. But the steam in this pipe had escaped at its weakest point — the family. Family members irritate and disappoint each other so regularly that they easily take the hit for whatever else goes wrong in our lives.

When I was done shrieking at my husband and son, I stormed up to bed and slammed the door, dooming myself to a night of wrestling with the covers and with my conscience. The next morning my family tiptoed around as if I'd buried land mines under the floorboards.

I went to work and, having punished all the wrong people, I spent the day apologizing to all the wrong people. Co-workers would ask, without really wanting to know, how I was, and they would find themselves listening to my confession.

"OK, I guess. God, did I scream at my family last night."

I must have told my story to a dozen people, looking for absolution. I hoped that if I repeated it enough times to enough people, I could diminish it or give it away.

"Buy gifts," my friend Catherine said, suggesting an act of penance. "That's what I always do."

My son called me when he arrived home from school, "Are you OK today?" he asked, and heat rushed up my neck and into my face.

Having modeled the wrong behavior the night before, I attempted to model the right behavior now.

"I'm sorry," I said. "I was mad at somebody else and since I didn't have the courage to yell at him, I yelled at you and Dad. It was wrong of me to lash out at you because someone else hurt my feelings.

"Although you could lock the door, you know. Where do you think we live? In Amish country?"

I could hear him smiling over the phone. "It's OK, Mom. Dad and I sat down and figured it out. Try to have a better day."

The heavens opened and the light of forgiveness shone down upon me, but it did not cure my emotional hangover. Even the blessings of the ones you love cannot clear a head stuffy with regret.

There is no home remedy for emotional hangovers. No hair of the dog that bit you. Only time cures an emotional hangover.

Each night you sleep a little deeper. Each morning you wake and remember a little less.

# This is the life

ON THE COVER of this month's *Money* magazine is a little girl on a tire swing. She's swinging in Nashua, N.H., *Money* magazine's 11th annual Best Place to Live in America.

Nashua was also *Money's* first Best Place to Live in America, in 1987, but tumbled down the list when the mills closed. Techno industries filled the economic void and returned Nashua to the top of the 300 metropolitan areas surveyed this year.

For the sake of comparison, Baltimore is No. 156 on the list, down from 91st last year, and Hagerstown climbed from 139th to 129th. Those poor people in Davenport, Iowa, must be feeling terrible right now. Their town finished dead last: No. 300.

How does one determine what town is the Best Place to Live in America?

As you might expect from a magazine named *Money*, economic issues are weighted heavily in the complex formula the editors use: employment, housing costs, affordable medical care and taxes.

But, driven by their readers, *Money* also includes such things as number of sunny days and proximity to skiing. "Close to relatives" is also a factor, but it isn't clear whether that is a positive or negative.

According to the editors, crime and safety were most important to the magazine's readers in evaluating places to live, followed by clean water. Predictably, women rated museums and symphonies highly, and men favored a town with sports teams.

*Money* didn't ask my opinion on the best place to live — indeed, the people I live with don't want to know what I think — but I have generated my own criteria for the Best Place to Live in America. Number of sunny days is right up there for me, too. But there are other indexes on which I would rely.

Ease of commuting was important in *Money's* Best Place to Live formula, but I'd like to live where you don't have to pay before you pump and where your husband can flick off another driver in traffic without leaving you a widow.

Cost of living was important in picking the Best Place to Live in

America, but I'd like to live in a place where there are no hidden cameras at the ATM machines. No ATMs? Even better. I'd like to live in a place with tellers who recognize you without an ID and who don't slip your change to you under an inch-thick Plexiglas barrier.

I want to live where a banana split costs less than $3 and where all the teen-agers hang out in the parking lot where it is sold.

One of Nashua's winning features is its proximity to the world-class medical facilities in Boston. I'd rather live in a place where you can run into your pediatrician in the grocery store and not feel bad about asking about the rash on your son's leg.

I want to live in a town where I will be buried out of the same church where my children were baptized and where the clergyman knows me well enough to tell funny stories about me.

*Money* magazine rates proximity to recreation — lakes, mountains and oceans — high on its list. But I want to live where the kids can ride their bikes to a pool and where the video store has copies of movies like "Enchanted April."

The cultural arts are important to me, too, just as they are to the women surveyed by *Money*. But I want the ticket to cost me $8, not the parking.

Low taxes are important to *Money's* readers, but I don't care what the taxes are if the street-sweeping truck passes through my neighborhood as often as a police cruiser. I want to live where people leave six-packs out for the garbage collectors on really hot days and where the letter carrier saves the free cereal samples that come in the mail for the little boy down the street.

I want to live in a town where everyone leaves his house key under the potted plant on the porch and where I know the paperboy's mother and where I can send my kids to the corner store for bread or milk before dinner and only worry about the candy they are going to buy with the change.

My husband says it sounds like I want to live in a town where Andy and Barney police the streets, where Floyd cuts hair and dispenses gossip, where Goober fixes cars and where Aunt Bea serves a hot lunch every day, with pie and coffee.

But I checked, and Mayberry isn't on the list of *Money* magazine's Best Places to Live in America.

# Chapter 7

## *True* Facts

# Hairy facts and other fictions

AS YOU READ this, I am in line at the grocery store with a shopping cart full of the ingredients for side dishes I have not made in a year.

It is a long, long line of women pushing shopping carts full of ingredients for side dishes they have not made in a year.

So, where there should be a column, there is nothing but ...

True Facts.

- Publishers say that women are the buyers of 70 percent to 80 percent of fiction titles. That is because they stubbornly cling to the belief that they will have time to read them some day.

- Voice mail was invented because husbands and teen-agers can't remember to deliver messages, even after they write them down.

- It is hard to tell which bath towels need washing when they are all on the floor.

- A Penn State researcher criticized the American Girl series of dolls because the books that accompany them ignore unpleasant historical realities. That's just what young girls need: unpleasant historical realities.

- Mothers carry tote bags because their children treat them like one.

- The White House orders an average of 200 pizzas every day — second only to the number ordered by my house during a single soccer season.

- A study conducted by the University of Maryland and Bucknell University reports that women are less likely than men to talk about their own achievements because they worry that other women would feel bad and not like them as much.

- The size of a woman's laundry pile is related to the ages of her children, not to the number of children she has.

- Nissan, the automobile manufacturer, recently launched a search for "Car Pool Parent of the Year." The criteria? "Someone who meets the needs of a rigorous car pool schedule with patience, good humor and safe driving." The winner was to receive a new minivan and all the kids she can drive.

- If your pre-schooler is in "time out" before 7 a.m., you know it is going to be a bad day.

- The *RoMANtic Newsletter*, a practical guide to resurrecting romance in your relationship, offers these tips for men: "Fax her a photocopy of your hand so she can 'hold' it; Use Rain-X Anti-Fog and a cotton swab to write love notes on bathroom mirrors; create a romantic screen saver for her computer, and eat Jelly Bellys blindfolded and try to guess their flavors."

- According to a recent study of consumer attitudes toward unwanted hair, 60 percent of men believe that excess body hair makes them feel more masculine. Only 10 percent of women agree. Furthermore, 67 percent of women say they are "really turned off" by hairy men.

- If your teen-agers ask to go to the library, you can bet they are studying the social patterns of the Homo sapiens. Kids don't go to the library for any other reason.

- Advertising to young people grew 50 percent to $1.5 billion between 1993 and 1996, according to *Competitive Media Reporting*. The reason? Children 14 and under have $20 billion to spend. And they all think their allowances are too small.

- Women live longer than men. One of the reasons? Women are more religious and more connected with family and friends and better able to handle the hardships of growing older. That, and they are still working on their list of things to do.

- Women go to bed every night believing tomorrow will be better.

And the truest True Fact of all: There is no flattery like another woman's scrutiny.

# The tape is rolling

THERE ARE THINGS in this life that are true. Absolutely true. Children think they know these things. Men talk like they do. But only women really know.

Here, then, is another glimpse inside the store of knowledge that has come to be known as True Facts. As always, I am grateful to those who have made these true facts known to me.

- Don't even look for the Scotch tape. Your children have already used it all up.

- "My mom lets me." The most common phrase uttered by a child to an adult not his parent. Almost always a lie.

- It is a common misconception that sleep-over means sleeping over at someone else's house. It does not. It means that after your child spends the night at another child's house, you have to do the sleeping part of it over sometime that next afternoon or your child will not be fit to live with.

- If you go back to bed after your children leave for school and ignore that ringing phone, it will be the school calling to tell you your child is sick and needs to come home.

- Where are all the spoons? Probably the same place all the other socks are.

- Old Russian proverb: Women do everything. Men do the rest.

- You know your child has reached adolescence when the field trip permission slips come home with "My parent will not be able to chaperon" already checked off.

- Only mothers put the caps back on the markers. That's because they paid for them.

- Men don't sing in church. Women would feel bad for the organist if they didn't.

- If your child has a sore throat and you take him for a strep test, he will not have strep throat. If you give him a couple of hard candies and send him to school, your child will have strep throat.

- Everything in your child's life should have a driver's side power lock — just like the ones on car windows and car doors.

- Why is it that you can't remember where you put your car keys, but you can't forget any of those painful grade-school injustices?

- Women don't read directions. Men don't ask for them.

- "I don't have any." Most common response by a child to an adult asking about homework. Almost always a lie, and you will find that out 30 minutes before bedtime.

- No matter how much laundry you do, the outfit your daughter absolutely has to wear is not clean.

- If your husband asks you, "Where do you keep it?" it means he wants you to go get it.

- If it is possible for your child to leave something at a friend's house — hat, jacket, backpack, toys — he will.

- Speed dial was not invented so that little girls who can't remember seven digits in a row can call their friends all afternoon.

- You are aging like your mother.

- Women bond around problems. Men don't acknowledge them.

- Let your neighbor put up the basketball hoop or the play gym. Then your children might actually use them.

- When the chorus performs at the school spring concert, your kid will be in the second row, all the way on the right, and her face will be blocked the entire time.

- The only time you ever lose weight is after you finally give in and buy something that fits.

- Every kid in the neighborhood is your child's best friend when you open a box of popsicles.

- Every year brings another body part to camouflage.

- It is bad enough when your son burps in public. But when your daughter does — and responds to your horrified criticism by saying that "all the girls do" — it makes you fear for the future of civilization.

• As soon as you save enough money to redecorate that room in your house, a car or a major appliance dies.

• Why are there never any Band-Aids? You know you bought some.

• No matter how much money you make, your credit-card bill is always a shock.

• There isn't a laundry detergent made that gets baby throw-up off your good blouse.

And the truest True Fact of them all: If you allow your child to push the grocery cart for you, he will run it into your Achilles' tendon.

# Shorter hair, longer days

TRUE FACTS ARE always true. They do not melt in the summer heat, and you don't have to water them. They are still true after a late-afternoon summer thundershower, and they are still true when the tomatoes ripen.

And they will still be true when the kids go back to school.

Here are more true facts from a woman's life. As always, I am grateful to the women who have taught them to me.

- Lunch is a nuisance meal in the summer. You never know what the kids will eat. And nobody — they in their play or you at your chores — appreciates the interruption.

- If you don't feed your children lunch, they are more likely to eat what you make for dinner.

- With each successive child, a woman cuts her hair shorter.

- "What if everybody did it?" is still one of the best responses to questions from your children.

- Women don't really feel invigorated after aerobics. They crave a jelly doughnut and a nap.

- Your mother knows how to push your buttons because she installed them.

- Air conditioning means your neighbors don't have to hear just how crazy your kids drive you in the summer.

- At first, you give your child a few tiny slices from your pork chop. Then you have to cook him one of his own. And before you know it, he will be 11 years old and asking you if you want yours. And you give it to him.

- A merciful God has provided every child with at least one parent who can cope when he has to have stitches.

- "When you are finished, please . . . " (choose one)

a. put the lid down;
b. close the door;
c. throw the wrapper away;
d. put the dishes in the sink;
e. clean up this mess;
f. go to bed;
e. all of the above.

- When a child asks for money, his father will reach for his wallet. His mother will ask, "What for?"

- None of those batteries you are saving works. Either that, or they all do and you don't know it.

- Nights out with your husband used to be so glamorous. Now that you have kids, you'd be willing to sit in the car in the driveway as long as someone else puts them to bed.

- Common summer resolutions parents make for their children: no TV. Read for a half-hour every day. Practice math facts twice a week. Pick up your room before any friends can come over.

- Those summer resolutions have the staying power of ground meat on the kitchen counter in July.

- Women with children put 20,000 miles a year on their cars — 1 mile at a time.

- Admit it. You have fed your children cereal for dinner.

- None of the pencils your children have used ever has any eraser left.

- Nothing makes you feel as good as an unsolicited compliment — for your child.

- Sixty-eight percent of women polled by *Redbook* said men ought to worry more about how they look in swimsuits.

- Author Scott Peck calls parenting "a lifetime of heartbreaking servitude."

- Phrases such as "make him pitch to you" and "wait for your pitch" are not meaningful when yelled to a Little League batter. The only thing a parent should yell is something truly helpful, such as: "Tie your shoe."

- Products women are waiting for: stain-remover stick on a rope. You could hang it around your neck, where it would be handy when your kids get ketchup on their sleeves or you splatter tomato sauce on your blouse.

- You know your marriage has reached a dead spot when your husband gives you a World Cup T-shirt because he really believes you want one.

- Kids hate it when you lick your thumb and use it to scrub food off their faces.

- The number of minutes you can do on a Stairmaster bears absolutely no relation to how winded you feel after carrying the laundry upstairs.

And the truest true fact of all: The more activities your children have, the more often you serve spaghetti for dinner.

# Two Happy Meals, hold the gum

IN THIS WORLD of shifting sands and shifting values, we need some things that we can count on to be true, always and forever. I am grateful to all the women who have made these truths known to me:

- When your children start eating two Happy Meals, it is time they graduated to the adult menu.

- Tell two children to get rid of their gum before going into church. The boy will either swallow it or drop it off the top of the three-story parking garage to see what happens. The girl will ask you to hold it.

- You have only received a really special gift from your husband if you feel like you ought to insure it. It is not a special gift if it plugs in.

- If you put something on the steps to go upstairs, men will walk past it 99 times out of 100. On their 100th trip up the stairs, they will call out to you, complaining that if you keep putting stuff on the steps, someone will fall and get hurt.

- If you want your children to put on their shoes for school, you have to start telling them the night before.

- When your husband returns from a business trip, he will be yearning for your spaghetti and time with the kids. You will want to eat anything at all that has not been cooked by you and is not shared with children.

- When your children begin participating in sports, you will seek for them the kind of coach who is a nurturing adult who can give them quality instruction they need to succeed. But after a while, you will not care who is coaching, so long as your child is on a team with the other kids in the neighborhood, so you don't have to drive to every practice.

- If your children go to bed with their pajamas on backwards, it will snow and schools will be closed. If you absolutely have to get to work, it will snow and schools will be closed. If you don't think you can get through one more snow day, and if your children are actually getting bored with snow days, it will snow and schools will be closed.

- Television sitcoms about families that include a sardonic mother, a zany kind of off-center husband and smart-mouth kids are not entertainment. It is not diverting or escapist if you live it every day. Shows such as "Dynasty," where everyone dressed for dinner, where breakfast was served from silver chafing dishes and where the mother rode horses for exercise, are entertaining.

- Clearly, only a woman is skilled enough to change a toilet paper roll, because no one else has ever tried to do it.

- It takes children longer to get out of the house in the morning than it took the United States to get out of Vietnam.

- If you are attempting to do anything involving tomato sauce, you should plan to change your shirt.

- The only purchases you should make at places such as Sam's Club are laundry detergent, paper towels and light bulbs — supplies that you will not abuse simply because they are in your pantry. You should never buy huge bags of blue corn tortilla chips or great big jars of salsa, because you will eat them.

- Immediately after you sign your child up for an activity that he requested, he will start complaining about having to go.

- If you are cooking something new for dinner, your children will not like it. Unless, of course, they do like it. Then they will hate it the next time you make it.

- As soon as you go into the bathroom, your child will come from miles away with either a serious injury or a burning need to discuss an upcoming social studies project with you.

- You can do almost anything — make beds, cook dinner, do the wash, supervise baths — while talking on a cordless phone. However, you cannot talk to your children while talking on a cordless phone, something they cannot understand.

- Your husband has not taken you out for a romantic dinner if you have to unwrap the food.

- You will work the phones for weeks to set up a baby-sitter for a Friday night, then you and your spouse will walk out the door and realize you have no idea where you want to go.

And finally, the truest true fact. It is easier to do it yourself.

# Slouching through

STAY TUNED FOR a holiday edition of True Facts.

Our guests today include Marie Osmond, Kermit the Frog, Miami Dolphins quarterback Dan Marino and the cast from "Les Miz."

This special was actually recorded in August with fake snow, fake Christmas trees and everyone sweating to death wearing ski sweaters in front of a fire while surrounded by brightly wrapped empty boxes. But that was the only time Marino and Marie were both available.

So, put another log on the fire, push the Christmas wrap aside and settle down for a long winter's nap and facts that are true any season of the year.

- A woman will carry two bags of groceries and a toddler up the front steps, but she won't carry a purse to a party.

- If teen-age boys did not slouch and trudge, they would not move at all.

- A biscotti is not the caloric equivalent of a zwieback. It just looks like one.

- You know you are getting old when your high school reunion is scheduled for the afternoon.

- Living with teen-agers is like living in a permanent premenstrual state. You are either irritable or you will be soon.

- As soon as you find your children's favorite convenience food on sale and buy 12, it will no longer be their favorite convenience food.

- The baby always wakes up the minute you pour the milk on your cereal.

- You know you are not getting out much when your cultural life consists of going to see children perform on a school stage.

- According to Harvard economist Juliet Schor, taking on a husband adds about five hours to a woman's annual household work time.

Helpmate is an oxymoron.

• One respondent to a *Men's Health* reader survey said, "The most important thing about sex is that it gives her enough energy to do housework."

• Boomers hate the term "seniors," so, as the first boomers turn 50, *American Demographics* magazine says publications targeted to older adults are using such euphemisms as "mature" and "prime" and coming up with upbeat titles such as "Looking Forward," "New Horizons," "Now is the Time" and "Young at Heart."

• You know you are not getting out much when the only reason you buy pantyhose is to have something to put over the hose from your washer.

• Demi Moore calls ahead to restaurants to make sure nothing she is served is cooked with cream or fats. I checked with Domino's and McDonald's, and they will not do that for us.

• A *Parents* magazine survey revealed that if husbands had more free time, 53 percent say they would spend it with their wives. The same survey showed that if wives had more time, 31 percent say they would spend it by themselves.

• Clothes dryers should have odometers on them so you can tell how many loads are left before they suddenly quit working.

And the truest true fact of all: If your children understood the lessons about money that you have been trying to teach them, you would not find so much of it in the washing machine.

# Chapter 8

# Sex, Drugs *and* Rock 'n' Roll

# Keep talking, because kids are listening

I RAISE CHILDREN for a living.

I interview experts on child-rearing. I read books written by experts. I go to workshops and conferences where I listen to more experts. And I stick my nose into the lives of regular parents to see how they do it.

Then I go home and try the stuff I learn on my own kids.

The next day, I come into the office and write about what happens when I do.

So you don't have to tell me that sex education is a lifelong conversation between parents and children, not a one-time, 15-minute talk before bed.

I know that.

You don't have to tell me that sex education is a continuing exchange between parents and children and not a lecture by mom or dad.

I have had experts tell me that.

I know that sex education is more than a plumbing lesson. I know it is a conveyance of values and expectations.

I read that in a book. I heard it in a lecture. I learned it at a conference.

But when I went home to try this out on my kids, I found that this conversation between us about sex and love and values is not continuing. It is not lifelong. It lasts as long as it takes my kids to walk out of the room in disgust.

I know, too, about "teachable moments," those times when an opportunistic parent will take the excuse of a question or a television program or a newspaper headline to talk about sex and love and commitment and values.

But teachable moments in my house last only as long as it takes my kids to mutter, "Don't worry about it, Mom," and leave the room.

How do you have these conversations with your children when they won't listen to you unless you're talking about what you are going to do for them next?

How do you initiate these casual but meaningful dialogues with your teen-ager when the only times the two of you speak is when one of you is raising your voice?

How do you convey values when you are both so prickly and irritable over the process of their growing up that you can barely stand to be in the same room?

How do you have a conversation when your child mumbles and mutters and grunts responses that could be called one-word answers if they were whole words and if they were answers?

(President Clinton had to get a pair of hearing aids because, his doctors said, his hearing had been damaged by rock music and campaigning. But I don't think President Clinton is hard of hearing at all. He just thinks he is hard of hearing because Chelsea mumbled answers to his question, "How was school today?")

I tried watching a sex education video with my children — because it seems they will watch anything that can be punched into a VCR — and as soon as they awoke to the subject matter, they got up and left the room. They were indignant, and acted as though they had been tricked.

It seems the only way I can talk to my kids about sex is if I tie them to a chair and gag them.

These lifelong, continuing conversations about sex, love, commitment and values do not take place in front of the fire with my son and daughter curled up in the crook of my elbow.

These talks most often consist of me following behind and yapping at them as they walk out of the room.

When I started this process several years ago, my children looked at me as if I were speaking in tongues. They were baffled. What was I talking about?

Now, they know. And they don't want to hear me talk about it any more than they would want to see me do it.

They are repulsed. Horrified. Disgusted. Embarrassed. They think I am ridiculous.

One is still staging weddings between her stuffed animals, and the other's idea of a wild night is a marathon Warhammer game with his buddies and all the Coca-Cola they can drink.

Neither one has ever been on the phone with a member of the opposite sex, let alone in the back seat of a parked car.

Am I nuts? they want to know.

Defeated, I did what I usually do.

I called an expert.

The people at Campaign for Our Children of Baltimore, which battles teen pregnancy with ad campaigns, has been talking to kids about sex for 10 years, through posters and television spots that are as hip as you wanna be.

"Will you talk to mine?" I asked. "Can I drop them off after school?" I wanted to know. "They learned about the plumbing in health class. So you just have to do the love, commitment and values part.

"Throw in some stuff about the deadly peril of unprotected sex, and I'll pick them up about 6."

Leave it to the professionals. That's what I always say.

Kristin Ditillo is one of those professionals. She is associate director of Campaign for Our Children, and her job is talking to kids about sex — and talking to parents about talking to kids about sex.

She said the things I have heard other experts say: Start early; don't wait for them to ask; listen to what they ask and give them concrete answers. (For the record, she also said sex education is a continuing process and a lifelong conversation.)

But Kristin Ditillo said something else.

"Parents often think their teens are just tuning them out and that their words are wasted. Wrong. Research shows teens do listen to their parents and want to know what they think.

"Don't give up," Ditillo said. "Even if it seems their minds are anywhere but on your conversation."

Keep talking. Don't give up. Even if it seems to you that sex education is you talking and your child under a set of stereo headphones.

Keep talking, because they will hear you. No matter how contentious your relationship is right now, you must believe that your words will touch their hearts and be written there.

Keep talking. Believe they will hear you. Because there is no other way.

# End of the innocence

"SO, YOU WANT to know about sex? I'll tell you things that will curl your hair."

That was my angry father talking. When my mother found my birth control pills that summer during college, there was quite a family explosion.

I was blunt and direct. They hadn't told me a blessed thing about sex during my entire adolescence, unless you count the little booklet my mother left on my bed, so they didn't get to jump in now.

My mother was grim. She and my father, she said, had not believed in any artificial means of birth control. They had relied on prayer.

"You had four children in five years," I said, my voice arching. "What was it you were praying for?"

The curl-your-hair speech and prayer-as-a-means-of-birth-control speech have long since become the stuff of laughing reminiscence at family holidays. The description of my father's face when he learned that the first of his four daughters had gone over the fence gets more vivid at each retelling. Even my mother is amused -- now that all four daughters are married and are done having all the children they want.

But the scene of anger and accusation that represented my first and only discussion with my parents about sex left a mark on me. I was determined that it would be different with my own children. All those years ago, I wondered why it had been so impossible for them to talk to me about sex.

Now I know.

When my son, then a second-grader, let slip some comment about "doing the nasty," I knew it was time. I bought the book (I always buy the books) "Where Did I Come From?" and we read it together. It is a slightly humorous cartoon depiction of the differences between men and women, the mechanics of sex and the development and birth of a baby.

I assumed a kind of science teacher persona — tab A in slot B, sperm meets egg — for that sex talk, and it went pretty well.

"That's gross, mom," my son said. But he has that greasy, grimy, gopher-guts curiosity of a little boy, and so neither of us was too uncomfortable. The subject did not come up again until Joe's sister was in second grade and he overheard some playground talk that made him think he had to intervene. "I think it is time Jessie read the book," he said, casting me his version of a knowing look.

I couldn't do it. I couldn't just pull my daughter up short and start reading her "Where Did I Come From?" I felt ridiculous, until I confided my profound but inexplicable hesitation to a friend and realized she shared it.

She told me about a note-passing incident at school that made her know it was time for "The Talk" with her 9-year-old. But just as she was steeling herself for this, she saw her daughter writing a thank-you note to the Easter Bunny and preparing him a dish of radishes.

"I guess I'll have to tell her about the Easter Bunny first," she thought ruefully.

That is the crux of it. We want to be open and honest with our children about power-packed topics such as sex, to tell them how the world works -- until we catch a glimpse of their innocence and it drains our nerve.

I was feeling foolish until Deidre Curry described a sex talk she had with her 8-old daughter, Tiffany. She is the education coordinator for Planned Parenthood of Maryland. She conducts workshops for parents on how to talk to their children about sex, for heaven's sake. And she, too, was struck dumb.

"I got to the part in the book that described intercourse, and I just stopped. I couldn't go on. I had to get up, go in the bathroom, look at myself in the mirror and say: 'Hey, you do this every day. Just do it.' I took some deep breaths, and I went back to her."

We feel like teaching our children about sex is an important part of our job, and we want to do it better than our parents did it with us. We are a little cooler and a little more frank when they lob questions at us. ("So," asks Joe, "how many times have you and Dad had sex?" "Twice that you know of," is my hard-eyed reply.)

But we are probably no better than our parents at knowing when it is a right time to bring it up. We forget that although we are worried sick about teen-age pregnancy and sexually transmitted diseases and haunted by the memories of love affairs gone wrong, all our children want are a few facts.

And for us to be there when they ask. And for us to listen when it is their turn to talk.

# That was then, this is now

MY HUSBAND WENT to college in the late 1960s, and he didn't do drugs.

He spent four years in the library reading back issues of *Sports Illustrated* and when he emerged from the stacks and graduated in 1969, wearing a sweater vest and chinos and a belt that matched his shoes, my husband was surprised to learn that some young people opposed the Vietnam War.

I left for Ohio University in the fall of that year and in the spring there were protests against the war and against the killings at neighboring Kent State, and Ohio University closed in a purple haze of pepper gas and marijuana smoke.

All these years later, my husband likes to say that I will never be nominated to the Supreme Court because of the kinds of questions they ask at confirmation hearings.

But I am not nearly as worried about the Senate Judiciary Committee as I am about the two relentless interrogators for whom I pack lunches each morning. They are daily battered with anti-drug messages at school and I am worried that they might some day ask me what I did during the Vietnam War.

What does the Woodstock generation say to the next generation about drugs? Or about sex, for that matter?

I do not know, but I need to think of something fast because I cannot wait until my children are packing for college.

The average age of first drug use has dropped to under 13, according to a study released last month by the Partnership for a Drug Free America, and marijuana use among teens has doubled to almost 40 percent the highest in seven years.

The study also reported that parents like me are as clueless about our children's access to drugs as our parents were.

If I am to believe these statistics if this is not an updated version of "Reefer Madness," kids are making decisions about drugs, alcohol and sex as soon as they have figured out how to work the combination locks on their middle-school lockers.

And that, I think, is part of the problem for those who believed that marijuana was no worse than a beer until they had kids. Our children will not be on the cusp of adulthood when they begin the kind of experimentations most of us outgrew.

They will be on the cusp of puberty.

They will not be sorting out these issues in the adult halfway house that is college where you can pretend to be grown up without actually growing up, but in our house, in their childhood bedrooms where we parents are still sometimes invited to snuggle.

And these decisions hold the potential for much greater harm today. There is not just pregnancy, there is AIDS and a laundry list of STDs that will leave a girl unable to conceive. And marijuana is reportedly 30 times stronger now than it was 25 years ago. Can you imagine being 30 times more stupid, not to mention hungry?

Do we offer our children our own example with the admonition that we were able to return to the real world, but some of our friends did not? That while these friends did not die, they lost their lives far worse. That there is no way to predict what will happen because drug use is a lottery system as surely as the one that decided which of our friends would go to Vietnam?

Or do we lock arms with the DARE campaigns in the schools, and deny, deny, deny?

Do we, knowing how kids love attention, manipulate the conversation, turn the dialogue around on them: "Did I do drugs? Why do you want to know? Is something bothering you? Let me hear what you think about all of this?"

The prevailing wisdom seems to be that parents should be honest with their children about their own drug use without either glamorizing it or demonizing it.

We are told that the children will respect our honesty and we will have the credibility to convince them that drug use is at least a waste of time if not an enormous risk.

Others equate such true confessions with the issuing of condoms at school. It is a mixed message of "do" and "don't" that confuses kids or worse, gives them a blessing.

My own conclusion is that the children we are trying to reach with anti-drug messages — middle-schoolers and younger — cannot begin to sort out the contradictions our own life stories would present to them. This is as true of our choice of a career as it is of our choices about drugs, alcohol, sex. It is simply more information than they can process.

Soon enough, they will know on some level if we are lying, if we are phonies and hypocrites. But when they are that much more cunning, they will be that much older. Perhaps then they can take in the fine points the lessons of our own lives offer.

The decibel level of the anti-drug campaigns in schools is so high that my children believe drugs will leave you drooling in a straitjacket if they don't kill you.

If they want to know more than that, for the moment at least, I plan to tell them, "Go ask your father."

# Carrying around a lesson

I AM THE PROUD grandmother of a 5-pound baby boy.

We call him Stewart, for Pittsburgh Steelers quarterback Kordell Stewart, in keeping with our family tradition of naming boys after famous Pennsylvania sports figures.

I believe Stewart's father, my son, Joe, was named after Penn State coach Joe Paterno. I am not sure because my husband, who chose our son's name, has never actually commented on its origin. When asked by friends if "Joseph" is a family name, he says, obliquely, "It is now."

Anyway, Joe is the father of Stewart, a healthy, happy, bouncing bag of flour.

Stewart arrived home from middle school wrapped snugly in a "Terrible Towel," a gold and black hand towel usually waved at Steelers games on third-and-long to great effect.

Because of the soft spot on the top of his head and the danger of spilling flour all over the place, Little Stewart was also fitted with a kid-size Steelers helmet, held in place by duct tape.

Little Stewart was Joe's first lesson in family life as seen from the giving end, as opposed to the receiving end.

He and his sixth-grade classmates were given bags of flour and told to care for them for five days, keeping careful records of the number of times the baby was fed, changed and comforted.

Little Stewart had to go everywhere with Joe, who was also instructed to plan and record quality time activities, such as reading or rocking or playing with toys. In addition, the students were permitted only 10 hours of child care during the five days.

On this point, Joe declared himself already a better parent than I. "You'd use up 10 hours the first day," he said in a highly inaccurate reference to my work schedule. But I did not take offense, because Joe was growing more and more irritable as he discovered the sacrifices of being a parent.

"I am trapped in this house," he howled. "I can't go anywhere without this baby." And I successfully restrained my impulse to tell my story of a baby boy who nursed every two hours.

"This is a ridiculous assignment," he continued at the top of his lungs. "There is no such thing as single fathers. Mothers always get stuck with the kids." And I decided it would be childish to grab the car keys and a credit card and disappear into the Florida Keys just to prove him wrong. Unfortunately, this assignment was an opportunity for a number of these sexual stereotypes to exhibit themselves.

For example, the girls dressed their bags of flour in adorable baby clothes, while the boys wrapped theirs in duct tape to prevent the spillage that might result from mistreatment.

The girls nestled their children in baby blankets and little wicker carry-alls while the boys carted their children around in the plastic grocery bags that are the scourge of recent anti-litter campaigns.

One girl decorated her bag of flour with synthetic corn rows and covered them with a cap of kente cloth. Another dressed hers in a frilly sunbonnet. One girl brought a change of clothes, and another had her aunt crochet a custom-fitted outfit for her baby.

I observed this with apprehension. "These girls are liking this assignment a little too much," I said warily to a teacher.

In contrast, one boy never removed his baby from his backpack and another left his behind, naked, in math class. That child was rescued and placed in foster care. It occurred to me that my son might have been right about single fathers.

"I wanted them to experience the immense amount of responsibility involved in meeting the needs of a child," said science teacher Sherry Ross.

"They said it was a pain; it was embarrassing. Not one of them said it was fun. Maybe this will give them a little bit of information they need to make decisions later in life."

Ross intentionally made her students single parents. "And they decided on their own that this assignment would have been easier with a partner," she said.

"I wanted them to understand that being a parent is a hard job and make their own connection to 'Look, you don't want to do this.'

"I told them when they are in the dark with a date and the pressure is on, I hope they remember back to Mrs. Ross' science class."

Will a long week caring for a helpless and dependent bag of flour serve as aversion therapy for sex?

I hope so.

But I worry that when hormones flood these kids, all they will recall is a distant and indistinct aversion to baking.

# She's gotta have it, too

ONE SATURDAY MORNING on the sidelines of a soccer game, where mothers keep one eye on the action while sharing their triumphs and confessing their failures to other mothers, a friend told me of the time she retrieved her startled teen-aged daughters from a parent-less house where they had been harmlessly hanging out with a couple of platonic male friends.

In the car on the way home, she tried to explain her caution to her outraged girls: "Look, you don't understand what it is like for boys. They will do anything, say anything to get you into bed because they get horny as hell."

My friend was stunned into silence by her daughter's response: "Mom, you don't understand. I get horny as hell, too."

It was a revelation to this mother, but it should be a warning to us all: Our daughters feel the power surges of puberty just as our sons do.

Have we forgotten this, too? Have we no memory of the pelvic buzz we felt when we locked eyes with the cutest boy in school? Don't we remember when we ached to be touched, to be kissed? Or when we were just plain curious to know what everyone was talking about?

Those feelings did not wait until our wedding night to bubble up in us. What made us think our daughters would not wrestle with them, too?

Fear, I think, has caused us to deny that these feelings exist in our daughters. Sex is less about good girls vs. bad girls these days and more about safety: from pregnancy, STDs, date rape. We can protect them better if we persuade them not to have sex at all — nothing beyond an innocent kiss at the doorstep.

As a result, the sex education of our daughters is woefully incomplete. We tell them how to have sex, but we don't tell them what would make them want to have sex. And we frame the entire discussion in the language of resistance: how to say no to a boy.

No wonder that when sex stops being icky and becomes something she wants, she is confused and ashamed. And a girl who is never given the opportunity to talk about those desires — to learn that they are normal and healthy, to learn what to do with them — may never take the next, most important step. She may not arm herself against pregnancy and disease because protection requires preparation, and that means she was looking to have sex.

The intoxicating feelings of desire — so new, so unpredictable, so frightening — are dangerous in young girls only if we do not help them to understand them and, insofar as they can, get a grip on them. If a girl does not know how to say to a boy, "Yeah, I want sex. I want it as bad as you do. I just don't want it right now, and I may never want it with you," she is handicapped, and it is our fault.

The sexual revolution has failed if we still believe that sex for girls is only about being in love. That's our old baggage. Sex surveys show that girls are having sex younger and they are having many more partners before marriage than we did. Surveys also show they believe that women are equally responsible for initiating sex, not only in established relationships, but also in new relationships. Girls today are adventurous in sex. They are more like the boys we demonize than they are like their mothers. How many times did we call a boy on the phone?

Today it is the rare young girl who will first explore her sexuality in the semi-adult world of college. The average age of the first sexual experience is 16 and dropping. And it is often true that she is having sex not because her boyfriend wants her to, but because her girlfriends pressure her.

You are nothing if you haven't gone all the way, her friends will tell her, even though most of them are boasting and posturing and lying about their own experiences. If it is difficult to resist the persuasions of a boy she fears will dump her if she does not come across, how impossible must it be to stand up to a clique of girlfriends who will shun her in a cold-hearted minute?

Add her own desires to these swirling imperatives, and it must be impossible for a young girl to say just who in the room wanted her to have sex in the first place.

How do we help her sort it all out?

"One of the problems for girls in the '90s is that sex is everywhere," says author Mary Pipher, who explained to us the pressures young girls endure in her best seller "Reviving Ophelia."

"They are constantly bombarded with sexual images. And they are constantly being told, 'Sex is great, it's sophisticated, it's fun. Go do it.'"

Because of how sex is portrayed in movies, television and advertising, young girls can easily conclude that couples go directly from a deep kiss to the nearest bed.

"Everything they see jumps to intercourse," says Pipher. "Kids don't have any sense that in this culture there are breaks and limits between kissing and having intercourse.

"This glut of sexual stuff has them so frightened that they stay away from the pleasant training period we had when we were growing up," Pipher says.

Sex is so stressful for girls in the '90s that it is often accompanied by furious chemical use. Only when they are anesthetized by alcohol or drugs can they face the terrifying combination of desire, fear of AIDs or pregnancy, and their need for love and affection.

Pipher, who, despite her success as an author and lecturer still counsels young girls as a therapist in her hometown of Lincoln, Neb., says the first step is to help these girls understand that in this sexually chaotic culture, the only limits are the ones she chooses for herself and the only ground rules are the ones she negotiates with her partner.

"That means you have to know what you want," Pipher says. "And you have to be able to explain your expectations to someone else."

"Kids can't imagine a conversation like that," says Baltimore's Debbie Roffman, who is in the trenches with kids every day as a human sexuality educator for several private schools.

She agrees with Pipher's ideas, but says it is asking a lot to tell kids to negotiate sexual ground rules when they have never seen it done in the pop culture that absorbs them. And when they don't know what words to use.

"We have to stop using 'sex' as short-hand for 'intercourse' and come up with a better definition," she says.

"Even phrases like 'making out' and 'fooling around' imply these experiences aren't real. They are meaningless, and we aren't accountable for them.

"And 'How far did you go?' How far did you get?' These are horrible metaphors. This isn't about how far you got. It is about how close you want to be."

Roffman presses the young people she teaches to define these sloppy terms, and through that process she helps them construct a continuum of intimacy from hand-holding to intercourse.

"Once you have defined sex as a range of behaviors, the question is not whether she should have intercourse, but what is appropriate at what ages and what stages of development and under what circumstances.

"Then," she says, exhaling in emphasis, "you can have a conversation about sex."

Getting there will be very hard for us.

The mechanics of sexual intercourse are easy to explain. "Don't do it!" is easy to say. Much more excruciating will be finding words for those feelings of urgency that won't send our daughters — and sons — squealing from the room in disgust.

If we only tell them how, we have done only half of our job, and we have left unspoken the best part: the language of desire, the language of intimacy.

# Motherhood

*is a contact sport*

# Touching moments

WHENEVER I REACH for my son, in an attempt to administer a hug, he snakes out of my grasp and says sharply, "Off. Off."

Whenever my daughter passes through the room, my husband reaches out to her, and, before he asks for yet another hug, she waves him away, saying, "Don't even think about it, Dad."

Occasionally, my tender-hearted daughter will sigh and stand still for an embrace because she feels sorry for us, but my son will not endure a hug without a promise of cash.

"This isn't a petting zoo, you know," he says.

I saw this coming long ago, this personal-space thing, this irritability at the touch of another.

And I asked my children to please warn me well in advance of my last hug, my last good-night snuggle. They acted as if I were crazy. Never, did they imagine then, would they not want me to stroke their feverish heads, scratch their backs or kiss them good night as they drifted off to sleep.

To my everlasting regret, I was right, and they shun me now. An embrace is not physical affection anymore, it is physical restriction. I might as well turn the heat up in the room. They can not breathe with my arms around them. It is as if my touch causes their skin to itch, and they writhe away from me, grousing irritably as they go.

And the rare kisses given me feel like butterfly wings against my cheeks. I am more likely to sense their warm breath than their lips. And these kisses are over so quickly, I think I have dreamed them.

Like most mothers, I have loved to touch my children since they were first placed in my arms. Their skin was as smooth as warm water, their hair as soft as a dandelion crown gone to seed.

I never tired of the miracle of how they felt to my fingertips, and that miracle renews itself at each stage of their growing-up. My son feels long and stringy now, all sinew, veins and bone. My daughter feels as soft as a marshmallow, as warm as a hot-water bottle. Kiss her and your lips sink deep into her cheeks.

When they were young, my children needed to feel me close to them, and each had an animal or a blanket to take my place when I rose and left them for my own bed. Now I, suffering attacks of insecurity as they grow away from me, need to clutch them in the night. But they don't want to comfort me, preferring to fall asleep on their own, sorting out the events of the day as they go.

Ashley Montagu, in his 1971 landmark book, "Touching: The Human Significance of Skin," wrote of "touch starvation," a failure to thrive among infants who are not stimulated and comforted by the touch of an adult. I am sure the reverse is true, too.

Much is taught and learned through the thin covering of our skin, Montagu wrote; and those deprived of touch, particularly in mother-child relationships, feel lonely and estranged.

I know just what he means.

Montagu pointed to the chimp and gorilla culture, where babies cling to their mothers all day. But my children watch the Discovery Channel, and they suspect that if they give in to my pathetic begging for hugs that I will trap them in my long arms and pick nits out of their hair all day. I am sure they fear that if they come close, I will pin them down with a big paw and groom their fur until nightfall.

But my children do not have a fool for a mother, and I scheme for hugs and negotiate for kisses. I am patient, and I wait for them to show weakness, wait for them to feel tired, a little sick or sad. Then I move in and wrap them in my arms, gathering up their long limbs as best I can and cooing softly the way I did when they were babies.

And before they can gather their wits to protest, I have hugged them.

# Acknowledgments

My husband tells the story of chauffeuring our daughter and her friends, and listening in on their back-seat conversation. When Jessie, Joanna, Emily and Sarah realized each had a mother named Susan, they became suddenly quiet.

"It was as though they were contemplating the fact that they were all in the same boat," he said.

All of us mothers are in the same boat, whether we are named Susan or not. I just get to write about it.

It is for that reason that I begin these acknowledgments by acknowledging the mothers who have contributed so much to my writing and to my understanding of my children: my fellow Susans, Susan Elbert, Susan Puddester and Susan Eckert, as well as Connie Reynolds, Nancy Lomneth, Diana Smear, Nan Jarashow, Betsy Dawson, Peggy Wooldridge, Linda Krone, Jeannie Mincher, Kathy Helzlsouer, Nancy Roberts, Mary Bronson, Nancy Anselm, Linell Smith, Joy Donlin, Jill Mihoces, Libby Patcher, Kim Marcum, Janice Hubbard, Catherine Cook, Suzanne Wooton, Deborah Banker and Patty Waldman.

Thank you all. I don't know where I would be — on deadline or in the dark night of the heart — if it were not for you.

My sisters are mothers, too, but they stand apart because of the crucible of my mother's recent death and the bond that experience forged among us. Cynthia Helzlsouer, Ellen Eshenbaugh and Elizabeth Olshenske — your friendship is my mother's last and greatest gift to me: Thank you.

To my friend and sitter, Grace Sagun, who for 14 years has made it possible for me to work and write, and to my children's grandmother, Vi Mihoces, who loves them so much and believes in them so completely that she sends report-card presents before the report cards have been distributed: Thank you.

To my first editors at *The Sun*: Retired sports editors Bob Maisel and Ed Brandt, who hired me and immediately began to send me to more grand events than the high school games I had been hired to cover, and to Cameron Snyder and Vito Stellino, who treated me as a colleague when we were all covering the National Football League: Thank you.

To my friend Jo-Ann Kaiser, who told me I should write "Members of the Wedding," to former *Sun Magazine* editor Mike Davis, who printed it; to former *Sun* assistant managing editor Marty Kaiser, who liked it, and everything I wrote after that, and believed, when I was not so sure, that I could write a column: Thank you.

To Ray Frager, assistant sports editor at *The Sun*, who edited all my early columns and this collection: Thank you. Any mistakes in this book are mine, because Ray is too good an editor to have made them.

To Robert Schrott, assistant director for News Research, the librarians and staff of The Baltimore Sun Library. Thanks for making me look so smart.

To Steve Proctor, assistant managing editor for features at *The Sun*, who once closed his office door so no one would see him cry over one of my columns, to former *Sun* features editor Lynda Robinson, who used to laugh out loud at them: Thank you.

And finally, to my husband, Gary Mihoces, and my children, Joseph and Jessica: Thank you.

Joe said once that I wouldn't have anything to write about if it weren't for the three of them. He is more right than he knows. My life would be more empty than this space without them.

*Susan Reimer*
*Annapolis, Maryland*
*February, 1998*

208